Triple Talaq

Triple Talaq

Examining Faith

SALMAN KHURSHID

OXFORD
UNIVERSITY PRESS

OXFORD
UNIVERSITY PRESS

Oxford University Press is a department of the University of Oxford. It furthers the University's objective of excellence in research, scholarship, and education by publishing worldwide. Oxford is a registered trademark of Oxford University Press in the UK and in certain other countries.

Published in India by
Oxford University Press
2/11 Ground Floor, Ansari Road, Daryaganj, New Delhi 110 002, India

First Edition published in 2018

ISBN-13 (print edition): 978-0-19-948740-0
ISBN-10 (print edition): 0-19-948740-5

ISBN-13 (eBook): 978-0-19-909325-0
ISBN-10 (eBook): 0-19-909325-3

Typeset in Trump Mediaeval LT Std 9.5/14.5
by Tranistics Data Technologies, Kolkata 700 091
Printed in India by Replika Press Pvt. Ltd

Contents

Preface

The genre of this book is an unusual one. People often write about great social and political events they have been a part of, or indeed, watched from a position of proximate advantage—what is described as the 'ringside view'. I have known of many such short recollections of authors regarding landmark cases, such as the late senior advocate T. Andhyarujina's account of his participation in the *Kesavananda Bharati* case,[1] brilliantly argued by Nani Palkhivala. The Constitution Bench sitting in the Triple Talaq matter—as it has come to be known—may not turn out to be equally monumental. However, in some ways, it nevertheless has enormous potential to make an impact on how Indians of all hues, especially Muslims, will approach the subject of political rights, particularly religious beliefs and constitutional guarantees of minorities' rights.

The flavour of public discourse in recent years, undoubtedly influenced by political ideologies whose fortunes have been on the rise, is beginning to get a bit sharp. Populism has greatly overshadowed the idealism of the spirit of Independence (hopefully only as a transitory phase). It is a moral imperative for people who believe in the idea of India to resist irreparable damage to the heritage we cherish and without which, no matter what the beliefs to the contrary, we will never be what we are and must remain. The building blocks of such an endeavour are numerous and the parts of the whole will indeed take enormous effort to put together. Yet each part is invaluable in itself and I hope that this saga—that of the Triple Talaq case before the Supreme Court—is and will continue to be one such part.

Interestingly, a constitutional case lasts only for a few hearings and is followed by written submissions, if they have not already been presented before the Bench when the oral arguments commence. But despite the time and the often combative exchange between counsels for parties, what happens in court is but a small part of what goes on in the world outside; indeed, even of what happens in court, only a small part is actually reported by the media and reproduced in the judgment. Understandably, there are constraints of space, time, context, and understanding; so, reproducing a virtual blow-by-blow account of court proceedings with a contextual gloss might be of help to larger audiences. It is with that in mind that I have attempted to write this book.

Religion has an interesting relationship with modern democracies: in Mexico, public display of religious symbols or even clothes is prohibited;[2] the US is a plural democracy but closely adheres to the 'In God We Trust' ethos, to this day stamping it on its currency; modern Britain reserves the post of Lord Chancellor for a member of the Anglican denomination. In India, we have been somewhat subtle in observing multi-faith pujas for important events, although under the BJP government that has changed to majority religion only. There is, therefore, an uneasy balance between secular and religious existence. But the Church–secular dichotomy does not work in India. To begin with, India is blessed with several world religions and therefore no single religious establishment can be the counterpart of the secular edifice. So, instead of keeping religion out of politics, we sensibly give equal respect to each religion. However, the question, as to what is religion, remains. One just assumes that religion is what people think it to be. The Constitution recognizes religion but fails to define it. We have not even attempted to consider ideas like Ronald Dworkin's 'Religion without God'.[3]

Judges often have to decide what 'religion' means for legal purposes. For example, the US Supreme Court had to decide whether, when Congress provided a 'conscientious objection' exemption from military service for men whose religion would not allow them to serve, this would also extend to an atheist whose moral convictions prohibited it. It decided that he did qualify for the exemption.[4] In another case, the Court, called upon to interpret the Constitution's guarantee of 'free exercise of religion', declared that many religions flourish in the US that do not recognize a god, including something the Court called 'secular humanism'.[5] Ordinary people, moreover, have come to use 'religion' in contexts having nothing to do with either gods or ineffable forces. They say that Americans make a religion of their

Constitution, and that for some people baseball is a religion. These latter uses of 'religion' are only metaphorical, to be sure, but they seem tied not on beliefs about god, but rather on deep commitments more generally. For the European Court of Human Rights (ECtHR), not only are religious beliefs protected in education but philosophical views as well—those that have attained a certain level of cogency, seriousness, cohesion, and importance; are worthy of respect in a democratic society; are not incompatible with human dignity; do not conflict with the fundamental right to education; and relate to the integrity of the person: 'a weighty and substantial aspect of human life and behaviour'.[6] The ECtHR interprets religious beliefs very broadly to cover pacifism, veganism, and atheism within its fold.[7]

The ECtHR quite succinctly captures the context of its wide interpretation of religious freedom in the following paragraph:

> As enshrined in Article 9 (art. 9), freedom of thought, conscience and religion is one of the foundations of a 'democratic society' within the meaning of the Convention. It is, in its religious dimension, one of the most vital elements that go to make up the identity of believers and their conception of life, but it is also a precious asset for atheists, agnostics, sceptics and the unconcerned. The pluralism indissociable from a democratic society, which has been dearly won over the centuries, depends on it.[8]

Hence, the phrase 'religious atheism', however surprising, is not an oxymoron; religion is not restricted to theism just as a matter of what words mean. But the phrase might still be thought confusing. Would it not be better, for the sake of clarity, to reserve 'religion' for theism and then to say that Einstein, Shelley, and the others are 'sensitive' or 'spiritual' atheists? On a second look then, expanding the territory of religion improves clarity by making plain the importance of what is shared across that territory. Richard Dawkins says that Einstein's language is 'destructively misleading' because clarity demands a sharp distinction between a belief that the universe is governed by fundamental physical laws—which Dawkins thought Einstein meant—and a belief that it is governed by something 'supernatural'—which he thinks the word 'religion' suggests.[9]

The Triple Talaq case offered the opportunity to consider the very idea of religion, but the Court thought it appropriate not to dive into a metaphysical or philosophical exercise, limiting its attention to what might be described as the layman's religion. Yet, somehow it seems that drawing distinctions between the core or essential part of religion and the peripheral aspect cannot be attempted without an understanding of the nature of religion.

Our Constitution is the original compact between citizens through their representatives in the Constituent Assembly that provides for rights granted to the State (the collective rights of society) as indeed rights of the citizen against the State. Somewhat later the idea of Fundamental Duties took shape, but conceptually that is an explicit expression of the rights of the State. Among the rights of the citizen identified are the rights to equality, liberty, conscience, trade, organization, speech, and the right to practise and profess religion. Interestingly, over the decades most of these rights have been amplified and expanded far beyond the pale of the language used in the Constitution, such as the recognition of substantive Due

Process. However, with respect to religion, the Court has been somewhat tight-fisted and treated it as a dimension of our national life that has to be tolerated rather than celebrated.

The best that the Court could do was to fall back on the convenient distinction between the essential or core part of religion and its peripheral dimension. In 1954, the Supreme Court said:

> What constitutes the essential part of a religion is primarily to be ascertained with reference to the doctrines of that religion itself. If the tenets of any religious sect of the Hindus prescribe that offerings of food should be given to the idol at particular hours of the day, that periodical ceremonies should be performed in a certain way at certain periods of the year or that there should be daily recital of sacred texts or ablations to the sacred fire, all these would be regarded as parts of religion and the mere fact that they involve expenditure of money or employment of priests and servants or the use of marketable commodities would not make them secular activities partaking of a commercial or economic character; all of them are religious practices and should be regarded as matters of religion within the meaning of article 26(b). What article 25(2)(a) contemplates is not regulation by the State of religious practices as such, the freedom of which is guaranteed by the Constitution except when they run counter to public order, health and morality, but regulation of activities which are economic, commercial or political in their character though they are associated with religious practices.[10]

This, of course, is a slippery slope—what the Court might think is not essential may indeed in the eyes of the faithful be critical to their understanding and their faith. When the Chief Justice spoke of the difference between faith and legal reasoning, he was intuitively expressing the difficulty that a judge feels in tackling the subject of religion.[11] The Supreme Court went through similar difficulties in *A.S. Narayana Deekshitulu v. State of Andhra Pradesh and Others*,[12] where Justice K. Ramaswamy stated:

> In pluralistic society like India ... there are numerous religious groups who practise diverse forms of worship or practise religions, rituals, rites etc.; even among Hindus, different denominants and sects residing within the country or abroad profess different religious faiths, beliefs, practices. They seek to identify religion with what may in substance be mere facets of religion. It would, therefore, be difficult to devise a definition of religion which would be regarded as applicable to all religions or matters of religious practices. To one class of persons a mere dogma or precept or a doctrine may be predominant in the matter of religion; to others, rituals or ceremonies may be predominant facets of religion; and to yet another class of persons a code of conduct or a mode of life may constitute religion. Even to different persons professing the same religious faith some of the facets of religion may have varying significance. It may not be possible, therefore, to devise a precise definition of universal application as to what is religion and what are matters of religious belief or religious practice.

He added that this did not mean, however, that it was

> [n]ot possible to state with reasonable certainty the limits within which the Constitution conferred a right to profess religion. Therefore, the right to religion guaranteed under Article 25 or 26 is not an absolute or unfettered right to propagating religion which is subject to legislation by the State limiting or regulating any activity—economic, financial, political or secular which are associated with religious belief, faith, practice or custom. They are subject to reform on social welfare by appropriate legislation by the State. Though religious practices and performances of acts in pursuance of religious belief are as much a part of religion as faith

> or belief in a particular doctrine, that by itself is not conclusive or decisive. What are essential parts of religion or religious belief or matters of religion and religious practice is essentially a question of fact to be considered in the context in which the question has arisen and the evidence—factual or legislative or historic—presented in that context is required to be considered and a decision reached.[13]

In the end, the main challenge for a Court is that religion being to most people a personal matter, it is difficult to justify the interference of a judicial authority and what seems to fall within a constitutionally protected individual right. In the words of Justice A.R. Lakshmanan: 'Subject to consideration of public order, health and morality, it is not open for anybody to question the tenets and practices of religion, however, irrational they may appear to an outsider [citing Seervai in *Constitutional Law of India* (4th Edition), Volume II, p. 1268].'[14]

Generally, there may be no problem about a matter of faith unless it impacts another person adversely, be it of the same faith or another. To what extent can society claim the right to impose its idea of the good life upon a group or individual? To what extent can the institutions of law insist that a choice made by members of a group or community can be said to be lacking in the element of free choice or be considered unconscionable and therefore not deserving of protection? Is religion about an abstract idea of God or some other force that is protected from the interference by other institutions? Attempts in the Soviet Union to repress and eradicate religion proved unsuccessful when the disintegration of the Soviet State saw religion sprout in myriad forms, particularly in the Central Asian Republics.

Before we go any further, I must thank those whose efforts contributed to the birth of this book. The idea of the book itself was persuasively pushed by my colleague Dr Lokendra Malik who accompanied me to Oxford University Press for a talk on triple talaq. It was an impressively large gathering of editorial and marketing staff, not to speak of some exceptionally bright young ladies who showed incredible interest in the subject. The Q&A session that lasted over half an hour gave interesting insights about hazy notions regarding divorce in Islam even among well-informed young professionals. In preparing for arguments in the *Triple Talaq* matter, I was ably assisted by the many enthusiastic young associates in my chambers and our discussions over lunches, as indeed other meetings, were most rewarding. Each of them provided further support by dutifully turning up in Court, despite the Bench sitting in the vacation. Some, such as Azra Rehman, provided invaluable food for thought through their own research and personal points of view. The young interns who spent the weeks with us in chambers as we prepared for the case and went into battle, too, were very supportive and eager observers of the moments of challenge. I thus deem it important to recognize their contribution. However, three members of our chamber in particular worked closely on the case with me, furnishing me with innumerable articles from journals, authorities from several countries, original texts of the Holy Quran and important Hadith as well as commentaries. Sanchita Ain, Antony Julian, and my son, Zafar Khurshid, who recently returned from Oxford, all worked tirelessly to meet tight schedules and demanding hours in attempting to address the Bench on this complicated and vast issue.

Introduction

This is the story of the *triple talaq* judgment of the Supreme Court—*Shayara Bano v. Union of India,*[1] the lead case amongst several cases—written even as the Constitution Bench headed by Chief Justice Khehar, as His Lordship then was, reserved orders to consider the compelling arguments placed before it in the first week of the summer vacation in 2017. The then Chief Justice, who was to retire a short while after the summer recess, made a determined effort to get through some challenging issues pending before the Court. It is written because it is important for people to know how the Supreme Court decides such cases of great public importance, and indeed, what it is that it decides. After all, people's lives depend on what the Court decides. And there are always people on hand who selectively choose aspects of the judgments to advance some political goal, which occurred after this judgment as well. In a sense, this is also an effort to demystify the most powerful Court of the world. The judgment will, of course, be read and re-read by lawyers and people affected but, like this work, it can neither be, nor indeed is, a thesis on Islam. In recent years, perhaps as the outcome of intensely divisive politics, a growing number of people have misgivings about Islam and surprisingly many educated Muslims are not well versed with finer details to hold their own in a public debate. Perhaps this judgment, building upon the earlier one of Justice Badar Ahmed (as His Lordship then was) of the High Court of Delhi in the *Masroor Ahmed* case,[2] will somewhat clear the air. However, there is much that remains untouched for the present, such as *nikah halala* and polygamy, both of which are grievously misunderstood and perhaps even misused, and both of which the Court left for consideration at a later date. Finally, there is the issue of the Uniform Civil Code, at present with the Law Commission of India, and seen by its ardent advocates as a panacea of many social ills in our society (although minorities fear it to be the final undoing of their identity). The Uniform Civil Code reared its head a few times during the hearings, both implicitly and explicitly, and so it would be safe to say that the powers that be certainly saw the fate of the two to be linked.

India is going through challenging times. The idea of India, taken for granted by people for the many decades since Independence, is under severe scrutiny—some might even say it is under stressful attack. Debate itself, far less dissent, is being linked with ambiguity or apathy towards national purpose and patriotism. Vile and questionable actions are either being overlooked, or worse, being applauded as retribution. Many sensible people felt perhaps this was the opportune moment for the public dissection of contested notions of justice and religious rights. Yet one can see that the government of the day, not to be outpaced by street vigilantes, is making a concerted effort to put its stamp on the social and political structures of the country. Indian polity, some believe, might have changed irreversibly. But it is still too early to predict whether we are in for a fundamental redefinition of our national beliefs and aspirations or even a march towards a reality that will reject secularism and tolerance as we have known it for years. Yet, in the stormy sea of uncertain public opinion, it is reassuring to find oneself before the Supreme Court of India, an island of relative calm and security.

When early in 2017 the various pending matters began to be mentioned before the Chief Justice by lawyers representing women aggrieved by the practice of triple talaq, as well the All India Muslim Women's Personal Law Board (AIMWPLB), there were clear indications that the Court would find a slot in the near future. At one stage when the Chief Justice of India (CJI) suggested that a Constitutional Bench could hear it during the summer vacation, the Attorney General inexplicably indicated a reluctance to have the matter expedited. But the CJI was determined to take up the thorny issue. He was obviously determined to clear the decks as it were, having at one stage suggested that the Babri Masjid–Ram Janambhoomi dispute be settled through mediation, and even offered to attempt it if the parties were willing. I thought that was both generous and courageous, particularly as he made it clear that he would recuse himself from the Bench. Surprisingly, the reaction of concerned parties was somewhat cynical, as though it would take bite out of the bark.

I was initially asked by some members of the All India Muslim Personal Law Board ('the Board') to give my consent to represent them in the matter. There were several junior counsels already part of their team, which included Syed Naushad, Aijaz, Imtiaz Ahmed, Ahmed Syed Shakil, and so on, and I joined them for a couple of joint meetings to draft a response. My considered opinion has consistently been that the defence of Personal Law on moral and constitutional grounds is imperative but what Personal Law exactly is needs serious consideration. The legal strategy of the Board was largely devised by Imtiaz Ahmed (advocate from Delhi), Maulana Fazal Raheem Mujaddidi, S.M. Hilal, Tahir Hakeem (advocate from Gujarat), P.K. Ibraheem (advocate from Kerela), as well as Maulana Wali Rahmani, Kamaal Faruqui, senior advocate Yusuf Muchhala, Aijaz Maqbool, and Ahmed Syed Shakil. After our meetings, Maulana Wali Rahmani prevailed upon the Board to brief another senior advocate and approached Kapil Sibal, who had initially shown little interest in the matter but was persuaded to accept the brief the second time around. True to their style, the Board did not feel obliged to tell me that they did not require my services.

Here I might note that there was an event not long prior that was made relevant in light of the decision of the Board. It related to a request being made by briefing counsel Irshad Ahmed in the matter of the right to sport a beard in the Indian Air Force. I had just returned from a trip to the University of Oxford on the morning when the matter was called before the Bench of the then Chief Justice T.S. Thakur, Justice D.Y. Chandrachud, and

Justice L. Nageswara Rao. The case involved a junior commission officer being asked to refrain from keeping a beard that he did not have when he joined the force (since he was very young at the time). Essentially, the Court wanted to know if keeping a beard was mandatory for Muslims. I was conscious that I was arguing in favour of the beard without sporting one myself and as I looked around the courtroom, I saw several Muslim colleagues similarly bereft of beards (although my advocate-on-record fortunately did have one). I attempted to answer the Court's direct question about whether a beard is compulsory in Islam by honestly admitting that it is not to be found in the Holy Quran but there are several detailed references in the Hadith, thus making it a Sunna that is to be followed by all faithful as desirable and aspirational. My impression was that this was enough. However, when the judgment was pronounced on 15 December 2016, the Court held that no material had been supplied to show the compulsory nature of a beard in Islam.[3] The matter is now pending by way of a Review Petition. The Court had also observed that since the appellant had failed to challenge the subsequent termination of his service, no relief could be granted. In a later case where the same issue was raised, although only at the stage of mentioning for listing, the Chief Justice offered to pass interim orders for restoration of service if the petitioner was willing to abide by the extant rules of service on sporting a beard. The Court was perhaps influenced by the clear five tenets of the Sikh religion, as opposed to Islam where the five tenets do not include sporting a beard, although the Hadith provides for it. The present case, therefore, was an ideal opportunity to explain to the Court the relationship between the Holy Quran and the Hadith. The *Beard Hadith* case was decided by Chief Justice Thakur's Bench in 2016, the *Triple Talaq* matter by Chief Justice Khehar's Bench in 2017, and one expects that the *Babri Masjid* case will be decided by Chief Justice Dipak Mishra before he retires in 2018. Three successive Chief Justices with landmark cases in their tenures. It seems even the highest Court in our land adheres to the literary 'rule of three'.[4]

Courts, as indeed all concerned persons, need to get the right perspective on the contours of religion. This brings us to the core purpose of writing this book. As Romila Thapar has so succinctly commented in her book *The Past as Present: Forging Contemporary Identities Through History*, Semitic religions—Christianity, Islam, and Judaism (that is, Ahle-Kitab or 'people of the book')—are constructs that began with a single discernible structure at a determinable point in time and evolved in reaction to geopolitical events. Thus, many facets of these religions need to be understood in the context in which they emerged. However, unlike Hinduism, these Semitic religions, including Islam, relate back to a single sacred text or a group of texts regarded as a Canon. So, even if Islam is perceived as diversifying into sects and schools, it retains a particular reference point common to all sects and schools.

Sadly though, the Board seems least concerned about educating people about the idea of religion and restricts its endeavours to amplifying dimensions of religion on the assumption that no further conceptual exercise is necessary. So perhaps the Board's decision to 'replace' me with my learned colleague was indeed a blessing. I was no longer bound by the limitation of having to argue the

Board's brief, which was a relief. At the same time, it seemed a pity to let the opportunity go to clear the mist around Islam. This indeed should be the concern of popular religious institutions, but somehow, conservatives impose insurmountable constraints. Naturally, the protagonists would have assumed at that point that my role would be stillborn with their decision, knowing that it was unlikely that my convictions would allow me to take up a brief that opposed the protection of Muslim Personal Law. So, I imagine they were all quite surprised to hear that I had taken it upon myself to intervene in the matter, in person. For this I am grateful to the Honourable Chief Justice of India for accepting my Application for Intervention and letting me present my stand before the Court. In the media, it was reported that I was appointed amicus curiae in the matter. The truer story is that upon being asked by the Court which side I supported, I responded that I was offering an amicus brief without fully supporting either side. I attempted to explain the situation several times to the press, but it seemed most were little concerned with the difference. So, I left it at that, being clear that I had no personal brief to push. My only aim was to assist the Court in reaching the truth.

I

He Said, She Said, They Said: Arguments before the Court

The Bench that assembled to hear the matter on 11 May 2017, the first day of the vacation, was clearly carefully chosen: headed by the CJI (a Sikh from Chandigarh), it also had Justice Rohinton Fali Nariman (a Mumbai Parsi priest—something he reminded us all about during the hearing), Justice Kurian Joseph (a Kerala Christian), Justice Uday Umesh Lalit (a Hindu), and Justice S. Abdul Nazeer (a Karnataka Muslim). It is difficult to say if the Chief Justice chose the composition deliberately because the composition of a vacation bench depends to quite an extent on the availability of judges. Three separate Constitutional Benches were proposed for the vacations. Besides the present Bench, a second was to hear the *WhatsApp Privacy* matter and the third one, the issue of the *1971 Assam Accord*; thus the available pool would have been shallow. So, perhaps it was diplomatic design, perhaps mere coincidence. At any rate, the Court represented the plurality of the nation the best that it could. Though I am sure many would have noted that one segment was entirely unrepresented. At one stage when some light-hearted discussion was taking place about whether the Board was weightier than the AIMWPLB, I remarked that I was conscious of having to face five distinguished men on the Bench and to improve the gender balance the Court would need many more lady judges. That remark brought a response from the Women's Board suggesting the need to have a Bench only of lady judges! Some chuckled, others frowned, but none pressed the issue further. The task before the Court was a daunting one already, without the need to further justify the extent to which its representation emulated the nation or the parties before it. It was at this initial stage itself that I noticed that the Court was curiously proceeding without an appropriate published version of the Holy Quran. So, I asked my young colleagues to get enough copies of the edition for the judges as well as other arguing counsel. They promptly trawled the alleys of Daryaganj and picked up numerous copies, most of which have now been donated to the Judges' Library. And it seems the copy that I signed for senior advocate Anand Grover was so coveted that it disappeared before our side could conclude arguments. I wondered if that act too, like triple talaq, might be said to be good in theology but bad in law! There were other books that went missing as well, prompting a lady lawyer from western Uttar Pradesh (UP) to describe a grand conspiracy to remove them from the public eye. Justice Joseph quipped that God would ensure that the books reappear just as they had vanished. I am not sure if God intervened, but we did not hear the complaint again.

At the very outset the Court indicated that it would restrict itself to triple talaq and refrain from considering nikah halala and polygamy. The press reported that as though it was their final refusal and the Attorney General renewed his request for expanding the focus only to be assured that it would be taken up later, perhaps before another Bench.

The initial hurdle, as indeed the springboard, depending on which side one was arguing, was the combination of Articles 13 and 25 of the Constitution. There are several previous judgments of the Court that set the stage, so to speak. From the beginning the Court seemed to accept and proceed on the basis that religion is an established dimension of our national life that is recognized by the Constitution, even though the State has no religion and is secular, albeit that term is perceived differently from how it is understood in western democracies. Therefore, religion inevitably must be factored into any constitutional calculus.

The opening shots were fired by Amit Singh Chadha, senior advocate on behalf of Shayara Bano (the original Petitioner in the matter that came to be known as 'the Triple Talaq' case), hoping to take the Shah Bano saga to a logical conclusion. Curiously, Arif Mohammed Khan, who led the charge against the Board on the Shah Bano affair as a central minister, appeared on behalf of the AIMWPLB. Anand Grover, senior advocate representing Ms Zakia Soman, made a meticulously researched attack on triple talaq and relied on a variety of authorities, including case law from South Africa, to show the path to reconciliation between custom and modern law. The tenacious Indira

Jaising, senior advocate appearing for the Bebaak Collective, broadened the attack on behalf of women by questioning the seeming reluctance of the Court to question personal law per se under the Constitution. The Additional Solicitor General strove relentlessly to argue that the ambit of religion for the purpose of immunity from constitutional scrutiny must be limited to worship and belief while treating matters like marriage and inheritance as part of ordinary law. In a sense, this overlapped with the Attorney General's position, which implicitly (sometimes explicitly) was to prepare ground for a Uniform Civil Code under Article 44. To paraphrase my learned colleague, if the court strikes down talaq per se, the Union will 'bring a law' imminently. Whether one is already in the works or this was just posturing to assuage the Court against creating a vacuum, remains to be seen.

Indira Jaising argued for the primacy of Article 14 of the Constitution. It was her aim to negate the argument that the intention of the Constitution makers was to grant unregulated protection to personal laws. In her rejoinder, Jaising emphasized that, as had been shown in the course of arguments, repeated attempts were made in the Constituent Assembly to exempt Personal Law from the operation of Part III, or from the ambit of Article 44, which were emphatically rejected. Thus, it was the explicit intention of the Constitution makers to subject personal laws to State regulation. In particular, she relied on the words of the founding father Dr B.R. Ambedkar who famously said:

> The religious conceptions in this country are so vast that they cover every aspect of life, from birth to death. There is nothing which is not religion and if personal law is to be saved, I am sure about it that in social matters, we will come to a standstill ...

After all, what are we having this liberty for? We are having this liberty in order to reform our social system, which is so full of inequities, so full in inequities, discrimination and other things, which conflict with our fundamental rights. It is, therefore, quite impossible for anybody to conceive that the personal law shall be excluded from the jurisdiction of the State.

It was Indira Jaising's submission that Article 25 itself recognizes the difference between 'religion', which is a matter of faith or belief, and 'economic, financial, political, and other secular activity which may be associated with religious practices'. It was therefore critical to understand the difference between 'religion' and 'activity, which may be associated with religious practice'. The Constitution neither defines nor specifies the scope of religion. The Preamble of the Constitution uses the phrase 'liberty of thought, expression, belief, faith and worship'. It was submitted that the words of the Preamble may be used to interpret the scope and ambit of Article 25(1), which guarantees the freedom of conscience, and free profession, practice, and propagation of religion. This right is also circumscribed in the manner described in the Article. An example of the restriction on the right to propagate religion can be found in the anti-conversion laws made in the interest of public order. Her written submissions further added that, in any event, the Supreme Court has held that what is protected under Article 25 is the essential attributes of a religion and not every religious practice which is not integral to the religion. Thus, Personal Laws relating to marriage and divorce; infants and minors; adoption; wills, intestacy, and succession; joint family and partition pertain to activities which may be associated with religious practice, and may even have religious origins in their form and content, but this does not make them essential parts of religion. Such activities can be and have been regulated by the State.

The core of the Bebaak Collective's arguments was thus that, on a plain reading of Article 25, the right to freedom of conscience is subject to public order, morality, health, and the other provisions of the Constitution in Part III. The right must therefore be so interpreted that no right in the Constitution negates the other. Article 25 cannot, therefore, be allowed to trump the rights under Articles 14 and 15. They must be harmoniously construed so as to give effect to both. Any derogation from Article 14 cannot be justified with reference to Article 25. While Jaising was silently applauded for taking on patriarchal Islam, she soon dampened the spirit of the secularist lobby by suggesting that Hindu women also suffered immeasurable oppression and that too should be taken to task.

Arif Mohammed Khan too came in robes representing the AIMWPLB and must have been surprised that we were seated on the same side in the Court. The last time we faced against each other was on the *Mohammed Ahmed Khan v. Shah Bano Begum*[1] matter, when he was a junior minister in the government led by the late Rajiv Gandhi. He had taken a strident position in support of the Supreme Court judgment granting maintenance to a Muslim divorcee under Section 125 of the Criminal Procedure Code (CrPC). The position of the Board was that by divorce the relationship between the couple comes to an end and cannot be kept going even for the purpose of regular maintenance. In other words, the Muslim position was that whatever arrangement is to be made must be before the break is complete and final. Ultimately, Arif

Mohammed Khan resigned from the government and the Muslim Women (Protection of Rights on Divorce) Act, 1986 was passed. The Supreme Court upheld the validity of the legislation. However, the debate on *Shah Bano* was flagged somewhat unfairly as an example of Muslim appeasement by the Congress party. That perception continues to this day and has been built upon steadily to malign the Congress party and damage it greatly. It is a one-sided contest where Muslims often say that the Congress has failed them while the BJP merrily propagates that it is unduly tilted towards minorities.

Subsequent media interaction by Arif Mohammed Khan built on the theme that this matter had finally reopened the doors closed by Parliament in having reversed the *Shah Bano* decision. It is therefore important to place that case in perspective and explain why it did not figure significantly in the present matter. The matter was decided by a Bench of five judges presided by Chief Justice Y.V. Chandrachud. Shah Bano's husband, Mohammed Ahmed Khan, the appellant before the Supreme Court, had sought relief against an order of the High Court enhancing maintenance under Section 125 of the CrPC from Rs 25 to Rs 179.20. It was argued on his behalf that after the *iddat* period following pronouncement of talaq, he was not liable to pay maintenance. It is ironic that a paltry amount of approximately Rs 150 caused political tremors in the country, the aftershocks of which continue to cause distress even today. As considerable time has passed since the *Shah Bano* case and a misleading impression has taken root, it will be useful to revisit the case at some length.

The Supreme Court was to decide whether divorced Muslim women were entitled to the sustenance available under Section 125 of the CrPC and, in deciding that, to consider whether the payment of *mehar* was relevant to Section 127(3), which essentially clarified that mehar fixed to be paid as a consideration of marriage was often deferred indefinitely but had to be paid upon divorce. However, it could not be said that it was a payment upon divorce and therefore did not provide a carve-out from the obligations of Section 125 by virtue of Section 127(3)(b). Thereafter, the Court went on to consider as follows:

7. Under Section 125(1)(a), a person who, having sufficient means, neglects or refuses to maintain his wife who is unable to maintain herself, can be asked by the court to pay a monthly maintenance to her at a rate not exceeding five hundred rupees. By clause (b) of the Explanation to Section 125(1), "wife" includes a divorced woman who has not remarried. These provisions are too clear and precise to admit of any doubt or refinement. The religion professed by a spouse or by the spouses has no place in the scheme of these provisions. Whether the spouses are Hindus or Muslims, Christians or Parsis, pagans or heathens, is wholly irrelevant in the application of these provisions. The reason for this is axiomatic, in the sense that Section 125 is a part of the Code of Criminal Procedure, not of the civil laws which define and govern the rights and obligations of the parties belonging to particular religions, like the Hindu Adoptions and Maintenance Act, the Shariat, or the Parsi Matrimonial Act. Section 125 was enacted in order to provide a quick and summary remedy to a class of persons who are unable to maintain themselves. What difference would it then make as to what is the religion professed by the neglected wife, child or parent? Neglect by a person of sufficient means to maintain these and the inability of those persons to maintain themselves are the objective criteria which determine the applicability of Section 125. Such provisions, which are essentially of a prophylactic nature, cut across the barriers of

religion. True, that they do not supplant the personal law of the parties but, equally, the religion professed by the parties or the state of the personal law by which they are governed, cannot have any repercussion on the applicability of such laws unless, within the framework of the Constitution, their application is restricted to a defined category of religious groups or classes. The liability imposed by Section 125 to maintain close relatives who are indigent is founded upon the individual's obligation to the society to prevent vagrancy and destitution. That is the moral edict of the law and morality cannot be clubbed with religion. Clause (b) of the Explanation to Section 125(1), which defines "wife" as including a divorced wife, contains no words of limitation to justify the exclusion of Muslim women from its scope. Section 125 is truly secular in character.

[...]

11. The whole of this discussion as to whether the right conferred by Section 125 prevails over the personal law of the parties, has proceeded on the assumption that there is a conflict between the provisions of that section and those of the Muslim Personal Law. The argument that by reason of Section 2 of the Shariat Act, 26 of 1937, the rule of decision in matters relating, inter alia, to maintenance "shall be the Muslim Personal Law" also proceeds upon a similar assumption. We embarked upon the decision of the question of priority between the Code and the Muslim Personal Law on the assumption that there was a conflict between the two because, insofar as it lies in our power, we wanted to set at rest, once for all, the question whether Section 125 would prevail over the personal law of the parties, in cases where they are in conflict.

12. The next logical step to take is to examine the question, on which considerable argument has been advanced before us, whether there is any conflict between the provisions of Section 125 and those of the Muslim Personal Law on the liability of

the Muslim husband to provide for the maintenance of his divorced wife.

[...]

15. There can be no greater authority on this question than the Holy Quran, "The Quran, the Sacred Book of Islam, comprises in its 114 *Suras* or chapters, the total of revelations believed to have been communicated to Prophet Muhammed, as a final expression of God's will". (*The Quran—Interpreted by Arthur J. Arberry*) Verses (*Aiyats*) 241 and 242 of the Quran show that there is an obligation on Muslim husbands to provide for their divorced wives. The Arabic version of those Aiyats and their English translation are reproduced below:

Arabic version	English version
Ayat No. 241	**Ayat No. 241**, For divorced women
wa lil motallaqatay	Maintenance
mata un	(should be provided)
bil maaroofay	On a reasonable (Scale)
haqqan	This is a duty
alal mutta qeena	On the righteous.
Ayat No. 242	**Ayat No. 242**
kazaleka yubaiyyanullaho	Thus doth God
lakum ayatehee la allakum	Make clear His
taqeloon	Signs
	To you: in order that ye
	may understand.

(See The Holy Quran by Yusuf Ali, p. 96.)

The correctness of the translation of these Aiyats is not in dispute except that, the contention of the appellant is that the word "Mata" in Aiyat No. 241 means "provision" and not "maintenance". That is a distinction without a difference. Nor are we impressed by the shuffling plea of the All-India Muslim

Personal Law Board that, in Aiyat 241, the exhortation is to the "Mutta Queena", that is, to the more pious and the more God-fearing, not to the general run of the Muslims, the "Muslminin". In Aiyat 242, the Quran says: "It is expected that you will use your commonsense".

[...]

24. In *Mulla's Principles of Mahomedan Law* (Eighteenth Edn, 308), Mahr or Dower is defined in para 285 as "a sum of money or other property which the wife is entitled to receive from the husband in consideration of the marriage". Dr Paras Diwan in his book, *Muslim Law in Modern India* (1982 Edn, 60), criticises this definition on the ground that Mahr is not payable "in consideration of marriage" but is an obligation imposed by law on the husband as a mark of respect for the wife, as is evident from the fact that non-specification of Mahr at the time of marriage does not affect the validity of the marriage. We need not enter into this controversy and indeed, Mulla's book itself contains the further statement at p. 308 that the word "consideration" is not used in the sense in which it is used in the Contract Act and that under the Mohammedan Law, Dower is an obligation imposed upon the husband as a mark of respect for the wife. We are concerned to find whether Mahr is an amount payable by the husband to the wife on divorce. Some confusion is caused by the fact that, under the Muslim Personal Law, the amount of Mahr is usually split into two parts, one of which is called "prompt", which is payable on demand, and the other is called "deferred", which is payable on the dissolution of the marriage by death or by divorce. But, the fact that deferred Mahr is payable at the time of the dissolution of marriage, cannot justify the conclusion that it is payable "on divorce". Even assuming that, in a given case, the entire amount of Mahr is of the deferred variety payable on the dissolution of marriage by divorce, it cannot be said that it is an amount which is payable on divorce. Divorce may be a convenient or identifiable point of time at which the deferred amount has

to be paid by the husband to the wife. But, the payment of the amount is not occasioned by the divorce, which is what is meant by the expression "on divorce", which occurs in Section 127(3)(b) of the Code. If Mahr is an amount which the wife is entitled to receive from the husband in consideration of the marriage, that is the very opposite of the amount being payable in consideration of divorce. Divorce dissolves the marriage. Therefore, no amount which is payable in consideration of the marriage can possibly be described as an amount payable in consideration of divorce. The alternative premise that Mahr is an obligation imposed upon the husband as a mark of respect for the wife, is wholly detrimental to the stance that it is an amount payable to the wife on divorce. A man may marry a woman for love, looks, learning or nothing at all. And, he may settle a sum upon her as a mark of respect for her. But he does not divorce her as a mark of respect. Therefore, a sum payable to the wife out of respect cannot be a sum payable "on divorce".

[...]

28. It does appear from this speech that the Government did not desire to interfere with the personal law of the Muslims through the Criminal Procedure Code. It wanted the Muslim community to take the lead and the Muslim public opinion to crystalise on the reforms in their personal law. However, we are not concerned with the question whether the Government did or did not desire to bring about changes in the Muslim Personal Law by enacting Sections 125 and 127 of the Code. As we have said earlier and, as admitted by the Minister, the Government did introduce such a change by defining the expression "wife" to include a divorced wife. It also introduced another significant change by providing that the fact that the husband has contracted marriage with another woman is a just ground for the wife's refusal to live with him. The provision contained in Section 127(3)(b) may have been introduced because of the misconception that dower is an amount payable "on divorce". But, that cannot convert an

amount payable as a mark of respect for the wife into an amount payable on divorce.

[...]

31. It is a matter of deep regret that some of the interveners who supported the appellant, took up an extreme position by displaying an unwarranted zeal to defeat the right to maintenance of women who are unable to maintain themselves. The written submissions of the All India Muslim Personal Law Board have gone to the length of asserting that it is irrelevant to inquire as to how a Muslim divorcee should maintain herself. The facile answer of the Board is that the Personal Law has devised the system of Mahr to meet the requirements of women and if a woman is indigent, she must look to her relations, including nephews and cousins, to support her. This is a most unreasonable view of law as well as life. We appreciate that Begum Temur Jehan, a social worker who has been working in association with the Delhi City Women's Association for the uplift of Muslim women, intervened to support Mr Daniel Latifi who appeared on behalf of the wife.

[...]

32. It is also a matter of regret that Article 44 of our Constitution has remained a dead letter. It provides that "The State shall endeavour to secure for the citizens a uniform civil code throughout the territory of India". There is no evidence of any official activity for framing a common civil code for the country. A belief seems to have gained ground that it is for the Muslim community to take a lead in the matter of reforms of their personal law. A common Civil Code [the Uniform Civil Code] will help the cause of national integration by removing disparate loyalties to laws which have conflicting ideologies. No community is likely to bell the cat by making gratuitous concessions on this issue. It is the State which is charged with the duty of securing a uniform civil code for the citizens of the country and, unquestionably, it has the legislative competence to do so. A counsel in the case whispered, somewhat

audibly, that legislative competence is one thing, the political courage to use that competence is quite another. We understand the difficulties involved in bringing persons of different faiths and persuasions on a common platform. But, a beginning has to be made if the Constitution is to have any meaning. Inevitably, the role of the reformer has to be assumed by the courts because, it is beyond the endurance of sensitive minds to allow injustice to be suffered when it is so palpable. But piecemeal attempts of courts to bridge the gap between personal laws cannot take the place of a common Civil Code. Justice to all is a far more satisfactory way of dispensing justice than justice from case to case.

It is clear that the Court, although conscious that the government of the day did not intend to interfere in Personal Law, concerned itself with interpreting the amendment to the Code. Furthermore, it made an effort to examine the true intent of Shariah regarding provision/maintenance of a divorced wife. Just on that basis it could hardly be said that the CrPC overrides Personal Law. However, para 32 of the judgment regarding Article 44 would certainly have given the impression that indirectly the complete arrangement under Islamic law was given a go-by. As a consequence of the outcry that followed, the government of the day was persuaded to bring fresh legislation, Protection of Muslim Women (upon Divorce) Act, 1986.

This Act too was challenged—in *Daniel Latifi v. Union of India*, where another Bench of five judges, presided by Justice G.B. Pattanaik, interestingly upheld the legislation vide para 35 after considering arguments of both sides at some length:

6. The Statement of Objects and Reasons to the Bill, which resulted in the Act, reads as follows:

The Supreme Court, in Mohd. Ahmed Khan v. Shah Bano Begum & Others, (AIR 1985 SC 945) has held that although the Muslim law limits the husband's liability to provide for maintenance of the divorced wife to the period of iddat, it does not contemplate or countenance the situation envisaged by Section 125 of the Code of Criminal Procedure, 1973. The Court held that it would be incorrect and unjust to extend the above principle of Muslim law to cases in which the divorced wife is unable to maintain herself. The Court, therefore, came to the conclusion that if the divorced wife is able to maintain herself, the husband's liability ceases with the expiration of the period of iddat but if she is unable to maintain herself after the period of iddat, she is entitled to have recourse to Section 125 of the Code of Criminal Procedure.

2. This decision has led to some controversy as to the obligation of the Muslim husband to pay maintenance to the divorced wife. Opportunity has, therefore, been taken to specify the rights which a Muslim divorced woman is entitled to at the time of divorce and to protect her interests. The Bill accordingly provides for the following among other things, namely—

(a) a Muslim divorced woman shall be entitled to a reasonable and fair provision and maintenance within the period of iddat by her former husband and in case she maintains the children born to her before or after her divorce, such reasonable provision and maintenance would be extended to a period of two years from the dates of birth of the children. She will also be entitled to mahr or dower and all the properties given to her by her relatives, friends, husband and the husband's relatives. If the above benefits are not given to her at the time of divorce, she is entitled to apply to the Magistrate for an order directing her former husband to provide for such maintenance, the payment of mahr or dower or the delivery of the properties;

(b) where a Muslim divorced woman is unable to maintain herself after the period of iddat, the Magistrate is empowered to make an order for the payment of maintenance by her relatives who would be entitled to inherit her property on her death according to Muslim law in the proportions in which they would inherit her property. If any one of such relatives is unable to pay his or her share on the ground of his or her not having the means to pay, the Magistrate would direct the other relatives who have sufficient means to pay the shares of these relatives also. But where a divorced woman has no relatives or such relatives or any one of them has not enough means to pay the maintenance or the other relatives who have been asked to pay the shares of the defaulting relatives also do not have the means to pay the shares of the defaulting relatives the Magistrate would order the State Wakf Board to pay the maintenance ordered by him or the shares of the relatives who are unable to pay.

7. The object of enacting the Act, as stated in the Statement of Objects and Reasons to the Act, is that this Court, in the *Shah Bano* case [(1985) 2 SCC 556: 1985 SCC (Cri) 245] held that Muslim law limits the husband's liability to provide for maintenance of the divorced wife to the period of iddat, but it does not contemplate or countenance the situation envisaged by Section 125 of the Code of Criminal Procedure, 1973 and, therefore, it cannot be said that the Muslim husband, according to his personal law, is not under an obligation to provide maintenance beyond the period of iddat to his divorced wife, who is unable to maintain herself.

[...]

20. In interpreting the provisions where matrimonial relationship is involved, we have to consider the social conditions prevalent in our society. In our society, whether they belong to the majority or the minority group, what is apparent is that there exists a great

disparity in the matter of economic resourcefulness between a man and a woman. Our society is male dominated, both economically and socially and women are assigned, invariably, a dependent role, irrespective of the class of society to which she belongs. A woman on her marriage very often, though highly educated, gives up her all other avocations and entirely devotes herself to the welfare of the family, in particular she shares with her husband, her emotions, sentiments, mind and body, and her investment in the marriage is her entire life—a sacramental sacrifice of her individual self and is far too enormous to be measured in terms of money. When a relationship of this nature breaks up, in what manner we could compensate her so far as emotional fracture or loss of investment is concerned, there can be no answer. It is a small solace to say that such a woman should be compensated in terms of money towards her livelihood and such a relief which partakes basic human rights to secure gender and social justice is universally recognised by persons belonging to all religions and it is difficult to perceive that Muslim law intends to provide a different kind of responsibility by passing on the same to those unconnected with the matrimonial life such as the heirs who were likely to inherit the property from her or the Wakf Boards. Such an approach appears to us to be a kind of distortion of the social facts. Solutions to such societal problems of universal magnitude pertaining to horizons of basic human rights, culture, dignity and decency of life and dictates of necessity in the pursuit of social justice should be invariably left to be decided on considerations other than religion or religious faith or beliefs or national, sectarian, racial or communal constraints. Bearing this aspect in mind, we have to interpret the provisions of the Act in question.

[...]

32. As on the date the Act came into force the law applicable to Muslim divorced women is as declared by this Court in Shah Bano case [(1985) 2 SCC 556: 1985 SCC (Cri) 245]. In this case

to find out the personal law of Muslims with regard to divorced women's rights, the starting point should be Shah Bano case [(1985) 2 SCC 556: 1985 SCC (Cri) 245] and not the original texts or any other material—all the more so when varying versions as to the authenticity of the source are shown to exist. Hence, we have refrained from referring to them in detail. That declaration was made after considering The Holy Quran, and other commentaries or other texts. When a Constitution Bench of this Court analysed Suras 241–42 of Chapter II of The Holy Quran and other relevant textual material, we do not think, it is open for us to re-examine that position and delve into a research to reach another conclusion. We respectfully abide by what has been stated therein. All that needs to be considered is whether in the Act specific deviation has been made from the personal laws as declared by this Court in Shah Bano case [(1985) 2 SCC 556: 1985 SCC (Cri) 245] without mutilating its underlying ratio. We have carefully analysed the same and come to the conclusion that the Act actually and in reality codifies what was stated in Shah Bano case [(1985) 2 SCC 556: 1985 SCC (Cri) 245]. The learned Solicitor-General contended that what has been stated in the objects and reasons in the Bill leading to the Act is a fact and that we should presume to be correct. We have analysed the facts and the law in Shah Bano case [(1985) 2 SCC 556: 1985 SCC (Cri) 245] and proceeded to find out the impact of the same on the Act. If the language of the Act is as we have stated, the mere fact that the legislature took note of certain facts in enacting the law will not be of much materiality.

[...]

35. In Arab Ahemadhia Abdulla v. Arab Bail Mohmuna Saiyadbhai [AIR 1988 Guj 141: (1988) 1 Guj LH 294], Ali v. Sufaira [(1988) 3 Crimes 147 (Ker)], K. Kunhammed Haji v. K. Amina [1995 Cri LJ 3371 (Ker)], K. Zunaideen v. Ameena Begum [(1998) 2 DMC 468 (Mad)], Karim Abdul Rehman Shaikh v. Shehnaz

Karim Shaikh [2000 Cri LJ 3560 (Bom) (FB)] and Jaitunbi Mubarak Shaikh v. Mubarak Fakruddin Shaikh [(1999) 3 Mah LJ 694] while interpreting the provision of Sections 3(1)(a) and 4 of the Act, it is held that a divorced Muslim woman is entitled to a fair and reasonable provision for her future being made by her former husband which must include maintenance for the future extending beyond the iddat period. It was held that the liability of the former husband to make a reasonable and fair provision under Section 3(1)(a) of the Act is not restricted only for the period of iddat but that a divorced Muslim woman is entitled to a reasonable and fair provision for her future being made by her former husband and also to maintenance being paid to her for the iddat period. A lot of emphasis was laid on the words "made" and "paid" and were construed to mean not only to make provision for the iddat period but also to make a reasonable and fair provision for her future. A Full Bench of the Punjab and Haryana High Court in Kaka v. Hassan Bano [(1998) 2 DMC 85 (P&H) (FB)] has taken the view that under Section 3(1)(a) of the Act a divorced Muslim woman can claim maintenance which is not restricted to the iddat period. To the contrary, it has been held that it is not open to the wife to claim fair and reasonable provision for the future in addition to what she had already received at the time of her divorce; that the liability of the husband is limited for the period of iddat and thereafter if she is unable to maintain herself, she has to approach her relatives or the Wakf Board, by majority decisions in Usman Khan Bahamani v. Fathimunnisa Begum [1990 Cri LJ 1364: AIR 1990 AP 225 (FB)], Abdul Rashid v. Sultana Begum [1992 Cri LJ 76 (Cal)], Abdul Haq v. Yasmin Talat [1998 Cri LJ 3433 (MP)] and Mohd. Marahim v. Raiza Begum [(1993) 1 DMC 60]. Thus preponderance of judicial opinion is in favour of what we have concluded in the interpretation of Section 3 of the Act. The decisions of the High Courts referred to herein that are contrary to our decision stand overruled.

However, the Court added that:

36. While upholding the validity of the Act, we may sum up our conclusions:

(1) A Muslim husband is liable to make reasonable and fair provision for the future of the divorced wife which obviously includes her maintenance as well. Such a reasonable and fair provision extending beyond the iddat period must be made by the husband within the iddat period in terms of Section 3(1)(a) of the Act.
(2) Liability of a Muslim husband to his divorced wife arising under Section 3(1)(a) of the Act to pay maintenance is not confined to the iddat period.
(3) A divorced Muslim woman who has not remarried and who is not able to maintain herself after the iddat period can proceed as provided under Section 4 of the Act against her relatives who are liable to maintain her in proportion to the properties which they inherit on her death according to Muslim law from such divorced woman including her children and parents. If any of the relatives are unable to pay maintenance, the Magistrate may direct the State Wakf Board established under the Act to pay such maintenance.
(4) The provisions of the Act do not offend Articles 14, 15 and 21 of the Constitution of India.

Ultimately therefore, the late Rajiv Gandhi was quite unfairly accused of Muslim appeasement given that the Court interpreted the legislation to have furthered the logic of *Shah Bano* rather than reversed it. Furthermore, the Personal Law Board did not think it necessary to question the judgment in *Daniel Latifi*. In essence, the Court found that maintenance during iddat and making of proper provision within that period was an answer to

Section 127. As a result, that interpretation ensures that a divorced woman is not left at the mercy of the world and at the same time, the Shariah injunction against any transactional relationship between divorced spouses was respected.

The principal objection of the persons opposed to *Shah Bano* was that once a marriage comes to an end, there can be no transaction between the erstwhile spouses. Having to continue paying regular maintenance would mean some relationship being sustained against the concept of Muslim nikah and divorce. But that logic also means that any arrangement within the duration of marriage and before a talaq becomes irrevocable is acceptable. Even sharing matrimonial property under force of law while the marriage subsists is consistent with Shariah. For all the effort that reformists have spent on running down Shariah, there is no explanation why the concept of matrimonial property (such as residence, vehicle, other moveable property, bank accounts, etc.) has not been advocated even though it is available in Goa. Furthermore, no one seems to have tried to gather data on the impact of the *Shah Bano* and *Daniel Latifi* judgments on the condition of divorced Muslim women. Be that as it may, *Shah Bano* remains a landmark along with the incident of the banning of Salman Rushdie's *Satanic Verses* to pin the false charge of minority appeasement on the Congress party. The latter was never challenged in Court, which indeed might have been difficult with the judgment on *Lady Chatterley's Lover*[2] remaining the law of the land.

After the petitioner's side, consisting of Amit Singh Chadha, Anand Grover, Indira Jaising, Arif Mohammed Khan, and a few others concluded, and I separately made my intervention arguments (altogether taking two days), the respondents' side took up their arguments. While there were many voices clamouring to contribute, it would not be unfair to suggest that the burden was taken up almost entirely by two senior advocates—Mr Mukul Rohatgi, the Attorney General of India; and Mr Kapil Sibal, for the Muslim Personal Law Board. Of course, Mr Raju Ramchandran, Mr Mukesh Giri, and others too made invaluable contributions. And while I have and will refer to the Attorney General's contributions briefly in this chapter, the primary focus is on the response of the Board. This is primarily because the Board seemed to be the sole proponent of the argument that triple talaq as an instantaneous form of divorce is valid under the Shariah, which is the antithesis of the submissions I made before the Court.

A word on this organization then before we proceed. The AIMPLB was set up in the year 1972 to be an authoritative body of eminent scholars (ulema) to provide guidance on and represent the opinion of Muslims on important issues. Periodically, some people have tried to steer the Board towards political parties, but fortunately its enlightened leadership has remained aloof and apolitical. The Board was very graciously headed by Maulana Ali Mian Nadvi of Dar-ul-Uloom, Nadhwa who was venerated the world over for his scholarship and humanitarian message of *Paiyam-e-Insaniyat*,[3] and is now led by Maulana Rabe Ali Nadvi. Of the 150 members, almost three dozen are women, introduced a few years ago to ward off criticism of being male dominated. The women members, although not very visible, are all very distinguished and dedicated to the cause of Islam. On the other hand, the AIMWPLB seems to be packed with women activists determined to challenge the dominance of men in the voice of the Muslim community. At one point they seemed not just to oppose triple talaq but talaq itself, an issue that fortunately went no further in light of the Court's mandate to address instantaneous triple talaq and nothing else.

I was surprised that in the face of the growing hype and forceful arguments from the other side, the Board was unwilling to sense the mood of the moment. There is a political establishment that has strong views on the unacceptability of diversity, particularly when it comes to affairs related to religion. It is another matter that we have an inspiring and forceful Constitution that guarantees diversity and pluralism as its basic ethos. But Constitutions and institutions are what people make of them. Given that many people find it difficult to distinguish democracy from majoritarianism and goodness from populism, inviting institutional responses to cherished beliefs was foolhardy to say the least. Triple talaq was never such an important element of Islam or a Muslim's *iman* that, in making the decision to actively defend it, we should have put the entire edifice of faith in peril. It is, of course, another matter that the basic principle of inviolability of Personal Law be maintained. Furthermore, when the entire Muslim world has done away with triple talaq, it seems strange that we were unwilling to accept the inevitable. It seems the Board could not grasp that one sometimes needs to concede a battle to win the war. We are all living in difficult times, but the Muslims of the world face special challenges from all directions, not the least from within Muslim societies. From the Arab Spring, Taliban,

Al Qaeda, Dais, Islamic State, Boko Haraam to Lashkar-e-Taiba, Jaish-e-Mohammed, and other so-called jehadi outfits nearer home, many groups within our worldwide community have brought ignominy to the religion of peace and endless distress to the average peace-loving, rational Muslim. At the same time the detractors of Islam get a handle with which to beat its followers. In these circumstances, the worst that Muslim leadership can do is to divide its own ranks for petty ambitions and lose the support of many non-Muslim well-wishers by refusing to engage in meaningful dialogue. The Chief Justice made a pithy remark relevant to this when the Attorney General stressed that the Court was the custodian of constitutional value. 'We are equally the custodian of minority rights,' responded the Chief. However, what rights minorities have is the perennial question that troubles all modern adjudication in the democratic world. Because of Article 44 of the Constitution, it is sometimes too easily assumed that uniformity is the ideal that we will one day achieve and indeed, the term Uniform Civil Code reared its head on more than a few occasions during the hearing. Being part of the Directive Principles of State Policy, it is prima facie paramount, but as courts have found in the past, it cannot simply override Fundamental Rights. Instead, the two have to be carefully harmonized. Surprisingly, it was not the Attorney General alone who explained that certain constraints had prevented Parliament over the decades from proceeding on Article 44. On behalf of the Board too, there appeared to be an acceptance of the inevitability of Article 44 being implemented; however, till such time, Personal Law was to be left undisturbed. Subsequent reactions, both of the Board's members as indeed their senior counsel suggests continuing confusion. A variety of motives remain concealed behind the cover of reform.

The brief of the Board was obviously a difficult one, with public opinion lined up against triple talaq. Yet, I was surprised that my friend Kapil Sibal began his submissions by stating a general proposition that Islam, like all religions, was a patriarchal system and thus inherently discriminatory. Upon my protesting, he quickly corrected this proposition and explained that what he meant was that most societies are patriarchal, which bleeds into the practice of religion, though not the religion itself. But then he went on to argue something even more contestable—that triple talaq was a matter of faith affirmed and anointed by 1,400 years of uninterrupted and open practice and belief and therefore it was not open to the Court to interfere with it, although the legislature in its capacity as a reformer could do so. I thought I found some echo of acceptance of Article 44 (Uniform Civil Code) with a plea that till such a code is introduced, respective religious laws be allowed to remain undisturbed. Kapil Sibal went further to emphasize that just as Hindus, as a matter of faith, believe that Lord Ram was born in Ayodhya, Muslims believe in triple talaq as a matter of faith! Yet the Board did not flinch in saying that it was a sin and that it was doing its best to weed out the practice—a practice that is somehow integral to the Muslim identity, but which they yet attempt to exclude, abrogate, and slowly but definitively end.

In their written submissions, the Board submitted that the Preamble of the Constitution clearly enshrines values of liberty of thought, expression, belief, faith, and worship. Further, Article 25 of the Constitution guarantees freedom of conscience and freedom to profess, practice, and propagate religion. Article 25 guarantees individual freedom of conscience subject to public order, morality, and health and to the other provisions of the third part of the Constitution. Article 26 of the Constitution grants freedom to every religious denomination or any section thereof to manage its own affairs *'in matters of religion'*. Interpreting the aforesaid Articles, the Supreme Court in the case of *The Commissioner, Hindu Religious Endowments, Madras v. Sri Lakshmindra Thirtha Swamiar of Sri Shirur Mutt*[4] has held that those Articles protect the essential part of religion and further, that when a question arises as to what constitutes an essential part of religion, the same should primarily be ascertained with reference to the doctrines of that religion itself. The Board further cited the Court's decision in *Krishna Singh v. Mathura Athir*[5] holding that the Part III of the Constitution does not touch upon the personal laws of the parties. Further, the Court also observed that the High Court, in applying the personal laws of the parties, could not introduce its own concepts of modern times but should enforce the law as derived from recognized and authoritative sources. It was submitted that since Part III of the Constitution does not touch upon the personal laws of the parties, the Court could not examine the question of constitutional validity of the impugned principles of Muslim Personal Law, that is, triple talaq in one sitting, nikah halala, and polygamy as followed by four schools of Sunni persuasion, namely Hanafi, Shafi'i, Maliki, and Hanbali.

I am not sure if the Board properly understood the implications of its arguments, but clearly there is a gap in the thinking of the Board and people familiar with the Constitution. It is important to record here that though there was no dearth of opinion on the side of the petitioners that the Board was a self-appointed NGO with no authority and right to speak for Muslims and Islam, I disagree with that proposition; despite being a private body, the Board is comprised of eminent persons of religion as well as eminent personalities. The various *maslaq*s are duly represented on the Board and their collective opinions are not to be treated lightly. And I stated as much in Court. But, of course, they are neither infallible nor final in the scheme of Islamic jurisprudence; their position, though influential, is not determinative.

The Board argued that in any event, the issues raised by the way of the petitions were matters of legislative policy and fell outside the sphere of the judiciary. Their written submissions pointed out that the court has already taken this view in several cases, including the cases reported in *Krishna Singh v. Mathura Ahir* and *Madhu Kishwar v. State of Bihar*[6], wherein identical arguments had been raised, that such questions do not fall within the ambit of judicial review. The issue to be examined by the court in the present matter had already been examined by this Court in *Ahmedabad Women Action Group v. Union of India* (the *AWAG* case).[7] In that case, inter alia, the following issues were considered by the Court:

(i) Whether Muslim Personal Law which allows Polygamy is void as offending Articles 14 and 15 of the Constitution.

(ii) Whether Muslim Personal Law which enables a Muslim male to give unilateral Talaq to his wife without her consent and without resort to judicial process of courts, is void as it offends Articles 13, 14 and 15 of the Constitution.

(iii) Whether the mere fact that a Muslim Husband takes more than one wife is an act of cruelty.

The Board submitted that while considering the *AWAG* case the Court declined to entertain the above-mentioned issues stating that these were matters wholly involving issues of State Policies with which the Court will not ordinarily have any concern, adding that the Court also held that these issues were matters which were to be dealt with by the legislature. It was further asserted that even prior to the decision in the *AWAG* case, in the matter of *Maharshi Avadhesh v. Union of India*,[8] this Hon'ble Court had taken a similar view. In that case, a petition under Article 32 of the Constitution of India was filed seeking:

(i) A writ of mandamus to the respondents to consider the question of enacting a common Civil Code for all citizens of India.
(ii) To declare Muslim Women (Protection of Rights on Divorce) Act, 1986 as void being arbitrary and discriminatory and in violation of Articles 14 and 15 Fundamental Rights and Articles 44, 38, 39 and 39-A of the Constitution of India.
(iii) To direct the respondents not to enact Shariat Act in respect of those adversely affecting the dignity and rights of Muslim women and against their protection.

The Court, while dismissing the writ petition observed that '[t]hese are all matters for legislature. The Court cannot legislate in these matters.'

The second arm of the Board's argument was around the question of whether Muslim Personal Laws can be tested as being violative of Part III of the Constitution, and whether the expression 'laws in force' used in Article 13(1) includes Personal Law. Here the Board emphasized the judgment of Justice Chagla in *State of*

Bombay v. Narasu Appa Mali,[9] wherein the following was observed:

16. That this distinction is recognised by the Legislature is clear if one looks to the language of S. 112, Government of India Act, 1915. That section deals with the law to be administered by the High Courts and it provides that the High Courts shall, in matters of inheritance and succession to lands, rents and goods, and in matters of contract and dealing between party and party, when both parties are subject to the same personal law or custom having the force of law, decide according to that personal law or custom, and when the parties are subject to different personal laws or customs having the force of law, decide according to the law or custom to which the defendant is subject. Therefore, a clear distinction is drawn between personal law and custom having the force of law. This is a provision in the Constitution Act, and having this model before them the Constituent Assembly in defining "law" in Art. 13 have expressly and advisedly used only the expression "custom or usage" and have omitted personal law. This, in our opinion, is a very clear pointer to the intention of the Constitution-making body to exclude personal law from the purview of Art. 13. There are other pointers as well. Article 17 abolishes untouchability and forbids its practice in any form. Article 25(2)(b) enables the State to make laws for the purpose of throwing open of Hindu religious institutions of a public character to all classes and sections of Hindus. Now, if Hindu personal law became void by reason of Art. 13 and by reason of any of its provisions contravening any fundamental right, then it was unnecessary specifically to provide in Art. 17 and Art. 25(2)(b) for certain aspects of Hindu personal law which contravened Arts. 14 and 15. This clearly shows that only in certain respects has the Constitution dealt with personal law. The very presence of Art. 44 in the Constitution recognizes the existence of separate personal laws, and Entry No. 5 in the Concurrent List

gives power to the Legislatures to pass laws affecting personal law. The scheme of the Constitution, therefore, seems to be to leave personal law unaffected except where specific provision is made with regard to it and leave it to the Legislatures in future to modify and improve it and ultimately to put on the statute book a common and uniform Code. Our attention has been drawn to S. 292, Government of India Act, 1935, which provides that all the law in force in British India shall continue in force until altered or repealed or amended by a competent Legislature or other competent authority, and S. 293 deals with adaptation of existing penal laws. There is a similar provision in our Constitution in Art. 372(1) and Art. 372(2). It is contended that the laws which are to continue in force under Art. 372(1) include personal laws, and as these laws are to continue in force subject to the other provisions of the Constitution, it is urged that by reason of Art. 13(1) any provision in any personal law which is inconsistent with fundamental rights would be void. But it is clear from the language of Arts. 372(1) and (2) that the expression "laws in force" used in this article does not include personal law because Art. 373(2) entitles the President to make adaptations and modifications to the law in force by way of repeal or amendment, and surely it cannot be contended that it was intended by this provision to authorise the President to make alterations or adaptations in the personal law of any community. Although the point urged before us is not by any means free from difficulty, on the whole after a careful consideration of the various provisions of the Constitution, we have come to the conclusion that personal law is not included in the expression "laws in force" used in Art. 13(1).

This view has been confirmed by the Court in the *AWAG* case discussed earlier in the text. In view of the position that provisions of personal laws cannot be challenged by the reason of Fundamental Rights, it was submitted that the Court could consider the constitutional validity of the principles of Muslim Personal Law relating to triple talaq, nikah halala, and polygamy in one sitting.

Further, in *Narasu Appa Mali*, Justice Gajendragadkar observed the following:

> The Constitution of India itself recognises the existence of these personal laws in terms when it deals with the topics falling under personal law in item 5 in the Concurrent List—List III. This item deals with the topics of marriage and divorce; infants and minors; adoption; wills, intestacy and succession; joint family and partition; all matters in respect of which parties in judicial proceedings were immediately before the commencement of this Constitution subject to their personal law. Thus, it is competent either to the State or the Union Legislature to legislate on topics falling within the purview of the personal law and yet the expression "personal law" is not used in Art. 13, because, in my opinion, the framers of the Constitution wanted to leave the personal laws outside the ambit of Part III of the Constitution. They must have been aware that these personal laws needed to be reformed in many material particulars and in fact they wanted to abolish these different personal laws and to evolve one common code. Yet they did not wish that the provisions of the personal laws should be challenged by reason of the fundamental rights guaranteed in Part III of the Constitution and so they did not intend to include these personal laws within the definition of the expression "laws in force." Therefore, I agree with the learned Chief Justice in holding that the personal laws do not fall within Art. 13(1) at all.

At the end of this spirited defence of triple talaq, the Board tamely filed an affidavit stating that it was issuing an advisory to all *qazi*s to persuade all marrying couples to specifically rule out triple talaq in their *nikahnama*s. A similar fatwa is reportedly issued by the Deoband ulema.

Surely a qazi, upon receiving the advisory, might ask why he is being asked to depart from a matter of faith. The adversaries of Islam might see it as a retreat that can be built upon if the right amount of pressure is applied. And if that is taken as the end of the matter, the fundamental question about the role of faith in constitutional adjudication will remain unanswered. Instead, the Board might have remembered the old Shakespearean idiom that 'discretion is the better part of valour' and chosen to fight another day. Clearly, the Board must learn to speak in a language that is understood by others, including ordinary Muslims, instead of alarming non-Muslims and forcing Muslims into self-conscious submission. Ultimately, the destiny of Indian Muslims must be trusted to leaders from within the community and those from other communities empathetic towards their Muslim brothers and sisters. I have reason to believe that the Board made similar mistakes in the follow-up litigation after *Shah Bano* and in the case of *Babri Masjid*[10] as well, but for now I have chosen to concentrate on the case at hand.

In the course of arguments, the Board resorted to distinguishing writings of scholars on the ground of the school they subscribed to and emphasized the Hanafi majority amongst Indian Muslims. Some texts were even dismissed as being the work of '*qadiani* authors'. This is a slippery slope that India has largely avoided, unlike Pakistan. Unity of the umma is central to Islam and is thus ordained by Allah himself in the Holy Quran. While there may be some value to deferring to the jurists of ancient times, when it is not unreasonable to do so, it is highly undesirable to dismiss entirely some that come after them; or indeed to go as far as saying that 'they are not even considered Muslims', as Mr Sibal attempted to do in court.

The Attorney General, who, in fact, opened the arguments for 'the other side', appeared to be taking the position that religion and the Constitution are two separate things and, in the ultimate analysis, the Constitution must prevail. It is only till the legislature steps in that religion can have sway uninterrupted, except where the courts find that an ostensible feature of religion is actually not religion at all. For this purpose, the abolition of sati was cited as an example, as indeed was the case of the *Tandava Anand Margi*[11] dance decided by the Supreme Court. However, in arriving at any conclusion, any proposition or practice associated with religion must first be examined to decide whether it is integral to religion merely a social extension, or even an aberration or adulteration. It is only if it is found to be integral and if it prima facie appears incompatible with constitutional values will the Court have to decide which prevails. It seems that such a situation has never confronted the Court. Religious and social practices that have been rejected over the years have all been treated as non-core parts of religion. Interestingly, while on the one hand, the *Tandava* matter was flagged as an example of judicial intervention to prohibit a claim of religious practice, on the other hand, the *Jehovah's Witnesses* case[12] was flagged for non-interference and respect for tenets of faith.

The sweeping use of constitutional values often made by judges of the Supreme Court, as indeed lawyers, to buttress arguments calls for closer scrutiny so as not to provide an easy alibi for controversial choices of majoritarian flavour. Ronald Dworkin therefore falls back on what he calls a moral reading of the Constitution.[13]

Constitutional lawyers and scholars have therefore been anxious to find other strategies for constitutional interpretation; strategies that give judges less interpretive power. For the most part they have explored two different possibilities. The first, and most forthright, concedes that the moral reading is correct—that the Bill of Rights can only be understood as a set of moral principles. But it denies that judges should have the final authority to conduct that moral reading based on their personal understanding; that the judiciary should have the last word on, for example, whether women have a constitutional right to choose abortion, or whether affirmative action treats all races with equal concern. It reserves that interpretive authority for the people. That is by no means a contradictory combination of views. The moral reading, as I said, is a theory about what the Constitution means, not a theory about whose view of what it means must be accepted by the rest of us.

This first alternative offers a way of understanding the arguments of Justice Learned Hand, a great American judge. Justice Hand thought that the courts should take final authority to interpret the Constitution only when this is absolutely necessary to the survival of government; only when the courts must act as referees between the various departments of the government, because the alternative would be a quagmire of competing claims to jurisdiction. No such necessity compels courts to test legislative acts against the Constitution's moral principles, so Justice Hand therefore thought it wrong for judges to claim that authority. Though his view was once an open possibility, history has long excluded it; practice has now settled that courts do have a responsibility to declare and act on their best understanding of what the Constitution forbids. If Hand's view had been accepted, the Supreme Court could not have decided, as it did in its famous *Brown* decision in 1954,[14] that the equal protection clause outlaws racial segregation in public schools. In 1958, Hand said—with evident regret—that he had to regard the *Brown* decision as wrong, and he would have had to take the same view about later Supreme Court decisions that expanded racial equality, religious independence, and personal freedoms such as the freedom to buy and use contraceptives. These decisions are now almost universally thought not only sound but also shining examples of our constitutional structure working at its best.

The first alternative strategy, as I said, accepts the moral reading. The second alternative—called the originalist or original intention position, also described by many authors as Constitutional Originalism—does not. The moral reading insists that the Constitution means what the framers intended to say. Originalism insists that it means what they expected their language to *do*, at the time when they wrote it—which, as I said, is a very different matter. And it seems many self-proclaimed 'originalists' themselves are unable to find it unnecessary to make a distinction. Even Justice Antonin Scalia, when he was serving on the US Supreme Court, was criticized for his headstrong 'originalist' position being somewhat conflated.[15] In essence, originalism posits that the Bill of Rights did not lay down abstract moral principles to be applied to the factum of the time, but rather laid down the framers' assumptions about those principles; a kind of treatise about how to correctly apply those principles in interpreting the language set down. So, the equal protection clause is to be understood as commanding not equal status but what the framers themselves thought was equal status, in spite of the fact that the framers clearly meant to lay down the former standard, not the latter one.

The Attorney General attempted to further make his case by citing two decisions of the Supreme Court. He emphasized how the Court in *The Commissioner, Hindu Religious Endowments v. Sri Lakshmindra Thirtha Swamiar of Sri Shirur Mutt*[16] laid down that only those practices which are 'integral to the faith' can get exemption from State intervention and what constitutes the essential part of a religion is primarily to be ascertained with reference to the doctrines of that religion itself. It was observed that the use of the phrase 'of its own affairs in matters of religion' suggests that there could be other affairs of a religious denomination or section that are not strictly matters of religion and, to such affairs, the rights guaranteed by Article 26(b) will not apply. He further cited *Commissioner of Police v. Acharya Jagdishwarananda Avadhuta*,[17] which held the following in respect of the meaning of the expression 'an essential part or practices of a religion':

9. The protection guaranteed under Articles 25 and 26 of the Constitution is not confined to matters of doctrine or belief but extends to acts done in pursuance of religion and, therefore, contains a guarantee for rituals, observances, ceremonies and modes of worship which are essential or integral part of religion. What constitutes an integral or essential part of religion has to be determined with reference to its doctrines, practices, tenets, historical background, etc. of the given religion. (See generally the Constitution Bench decisions in Commr., H.R.E. v.

Sri Lakshmindra Thirtha Swamiar of Sri Shirur Mutt [AIR 1954 SC 282: 1954 SCR 1005], Sardar Syedna Taher Saifuddin Saheb v. State of Bombay [AIR 1962 SC 853: 1962 Supp (2) SCR 496] and Seshammal v. State of T.N. [(1972) 2 SCC 11: AIR 1972 SC 1586] regarding those aspects that are to be looked into so as to determine whether a part or practice is essential or not.) What is meant by "an essential part or practices of a religion" is now the matter for elucidation. Essential part of a religion means the core beliefs upon which a religion is founded. Essential practice means those practices that are fundamental to follow a religious belief. It is upon the cornerstone of essential parts or practices that the superstructure of a religion is built, without which a religion will be no religion. Test to determine whether a part or practice is essential to a religion is to find out whether the nature of the religion will be changed without that part or practice. If the taking away of that part or practice could result in a fundamental change in the character of that religion or in its belief, then such part could be treated as an essential or integral part. There cannot be additions or subtractions to such part because it is the very essence of that religion and alterations will change its fundamental character. It is such permanent essential parts which are protected by the Constitution. Nobody can say that an essential part or practice of one's religion has changed from a particular date or by an event. Such alterable parts or practices are definitely not the "core" of religion whereupon the belief is based and religion is founded upon. They could only be treated as mere embellishments to the non-essential (sic essential) part or practices.

In short, an essential part of a religion means the core belief on which the religion is founded. In all fairness, the Attorney General belaboured the point that one way or the other, no one could be allowed to discriminate between two individuals, be it between Muslim men and women, or between women of different denominations or religions. He argued that Article 14 did not allow this, but the Court felt that the Article could be resorted to against State action and not against private practices. It is here that it became necessary to argue that by giving Muslim Personal Law statutory recognition under the 1937 Act, enough ground was made out for intervention.

But the moot question that remained untouched was as to what the 1937 Act did besides removing custom and usage that had over the centuries become grafted on to the pristine Shariah. In applying Shariah, was the Court obliged to follow any particular maslaq based on any principle of choice, such as the common maslaq of the parties, in which case there will be no problem, but what if they follow different maslaq? It seems that there is no escape from attempting to harmonize, just as Justice Badar Ahmed did in *Masroor Ahmed.*[18] At one point during his opening submissions when the Attorney General found that the Court was resisting his wide propositions about all forms of talaq falling foul of the Constitution, he finally rested his case with the plea that the Court may accept the judgment of Justice Badar Ahmed in *Masroor Ahmed* and simply 'read it down', that is, affirm the High Court judgment that three talaqs given in one sitting shall count only as one.

In the course of touching upon alternative legal regimes the Court, Justice Kurian Joseph in particular made enquiries about the implication of the Special Marriages Act and whether proceedings under it would have any impact on a person's religious beliefs. I responded that it was merely an indication by the couple that they chose to be governed by the general law rather than their Personal

Law, a choice that is available to all. However, it was a little more complex if a couple got married under Personal Law, such as through nikah, and then registered the marriage under the Special Marriages Act. I also pointed out an interesting, if moot, issue—would the children of the couple be irretrievably bound by the choice of their parents or could they opt to have rights of inheritance under Personal Law? Be that as it may, the regime of the Special Marriages Act and other similar legislation that applies to all persons is effectively the optional Civil Code available to citizens. There is no reported case of religious groups purporting to interfere with any such choice. The question is whether a person can, at will, pick and choose between what the general legislation offers and what Personal Law offers.

The brief that I argued, or indeed, that which was argued by Kapil Sibal, was obviously seen in public and by the media somewhat differently from the arguments of other counsel. Being in public life and associated with the Congress party, we are often put through special scrutiny for motives and intentions. I imagine Kapil Sibal took a pure professional brief, although I have to admit that mine was entirely an attempt to shed light on something that has a personal and intellectual interest. Some may question whether our personal faith added to or took away from our arguments. As far as I am concerned, it could have only informed my task before the Court. However, it was amusing to see that several times channels sought to bracket Kapil Sibal and me in one bracket—in support of triple talaq. On the other hand, some Twitter handles described it as a case of running with the hares and hunting with the hounds. Such are the travails of professionals who are also politicians, as opposed to professional politicians.[19]

There is another argument that was made by several counsels and repeatedly emphasized by the then Chief Justice and Justice Rohinton Nariman during arguments of the counsel. It relates to the impact of the Shariat Application Act, 1937 as well as the Muslim Women Dissolution of Marriages Act, 1939 and will be considered later in the book.

These, in brief, were the arguments made before the Supreme Court. In the next chapter I have diligently reproduced my written submissions before the Court (elaborating upon them, where I felt necessary in light of the questions and lacunae that made themselves apparent during oral arguments). These submissions set out the middle path for the Court between the sweeping reform that the Attorney General urged and the obstinacy showed by the AIMPLB—a path of least resistance and interference. True that it may leave some questions unanswered, as the Court itself admitted that it would have to. However, they will present the best if not the true answer to the question of triple talaq, on a true and correct reading of the Holy Quran and the Hadith.

One brief episode might be mentioned for its historical importance, although it made little impact on the case. I mentioned to Court that the application of Shariah under the 1937 legislation was expressly subject to the exception of agricultural property, an attempt by the Muslim landed gentry to preserve their hold over property. Justice Nariman commented at one point that this was because federal jurisdiction under the Government of India Act excluded agriculture and placed it as a State subject. Be that as it may, the right of a daughter under Shariah remains denied to her decades after the Constitution was adopted. One wonders why women's rights activists have remained blissfully oblivious to this glaring denial of rights. Or is it Shariah only when it suits?

2

Triple Talaq: Bad in Theology, Good in Law

Though matters of religion have periodically come before our courts, and often been decided in the context of Articles 25 and 26 of the Constitution, claims relating to Articles 14–19 and 21, besides the Directive Principles of State Policy, inevitably continue to be made. Growing concerns over issues of human rights and gender justice have increased the demand on courts to respond to new challenges. The slew of divorce cases involving triple talaq is part of that trend, and comes at a delicate moment in the life of our nation. Accepted wisdom on pluralism and secularism is being tested on the touchstone of peculiar nationalistic ideology. Suddenly, diversity as we have known for centuries is sought to be questioned, sometimes with fatal consequences. The Supreme Court cannot refuse to engage on the ground that the issues involved have political overtones or motives, but it might advisedly contain its scrutiny to narrow constitutional permissibility and for the present, refuse an invitation to examine broader issues such as whether personal laws are part of law under Article 13 of the Constitution and therefore subject to judicial review; or whether a Uniform Civil Code might be enforceable. In other words, if the immediate concern about triple talaq and the related issue of nikah halala can be addressed by endorsing a more acceptable alternate interpretation based on Shariah, it would be sufficient for the purpose of ensuring justice to all.

In Islamic law or Shariah, the answer to any question, solution to conflicting instincts, or resolution to an issue is provided for in the Holy Quran—that is the final word and rule of Shariah. There is nothing more to be done. When there is no clear guidance in the Holy Quran, theologians must look to the traditions of the Prophet or Sunnah as recorded in the Hadith. If no guidance is found even there, then we must refer to a general consensus of opinion or *ijma* (which the ulema might arrive at after closely studying the first two). If the resolution is found by ijma then that would become a rule of Islamic law. To this extent, Islamic law, like any other, is a living and evolving body of law. However, it must remain rooted in the original sources of the faith. To understand different concepts under Islam, it is important to appreciate the context in which these concepts developed and were handed down. One interesting dimension that needs to be kept in mind is that unlike the US Supreme Court, our own apex Court has seldom ventured into the philosophical minefield of defining religion. It generally proceeds on the assumption that we know religion when we see one, or at least in regard to the ones that are familiar to India. I tried to tempt the Court to look at an interesting book, *Religion without God*, written by Ronald Dworkin[1] a few months before his death, but could not get them to open up that vast field. In fact, even the famous judgment of Chief Justice J.S. Verma, as His Lordship then was, on Hindutva as a way of life[2] was not taken up by the Seven Judges Bench presided by the then Chief Justice Thakur, on the point that it was referred to five judges and it were some related matters about electoral law that had to be heard by five judges in the *Abhiram Singh* case.[3] But be that as it may, just as Hindutva is described as a way of life and not necessarily religion (at least until and unless the review before the Supreme Court succeeds), it could similarly be said that Islam too is a way of life. Undoubtedly, both Hindutva and jihad have lost their true meaning because political activists have sought to use the terms for their own ambitions. It is another matter if the Court will, at some stage, consider the concept of a way of life and to what extent that can find a place in the constitutional scheme.

For the present it might suffice to use a commonly understood meaning of religion as 'a set of beliefs concerning the cause, nature, and purpose of the universe, especially when considered as the creation of a superhuman agency or agencies, usually involving devotional and ritual observances and often containing a moral code governing the conduct of human affairs'.[4] In simpler terms, religion refers to 'a personal set or institutionalized system of religious attitudes, beliefs, and practices'.[5] Religions, therefore, relate humanity to what anthropologist Clifford Geertz has referred to as a greater cosmic 'order of existence'.[6] Needless to say, there are considerable disagreements on the definition amongst different civilizations.

Islamic Civilization: Reformation Through Religion

Islam, like any other religion, was informed by the context of the time that birthed it. As the first half of the sixth century drew to a close, Arabia had become a hotbed of political intrigue and skirmish. The safety and primacy of trade gave way to other priorities—supremacy and territory—ironically fuelled (as has always been the case) by the rise of the two other major world religions of the time and the region—Christianity (in the Persian Gulf) and Judaism (in the Himyarite Kingdom of Yemen). Thus, even though much of the Arabian tribes remained devoted to their multiple gods, the yearning for spiritualism and a departure from ancient 'pagan' theology was evident. The people of Arabia began to be swayed by the intellectual and spiritual developments of these 'alien' or 'foreign' faiths and the reluctance to convert soon waned as pagan values and vocabulary began to be replaced by Christian and Jewish languages in the region.

At this critical stage, the Quraysh, a monotheistic Hanifiyya tribe, was the chief tribe in Mecca—it played a primary role in the political and economic trends of western Arabia. To hold this position in the face of growing tensions, the Quraysh introduced the institution of 'sacred months'—where travel (and thus trade) routes were beyond reproach and an armistice of sorts was instituted. This was particularly key as Mecca served as the home of the Kaaba—a polytheistic shrine and home of the Nabatean deities Hubal Manat al-Lat—making it politically and economically significant in the region, as well as a popular destination for pilgrims.

It was in this important city that the Prophet Mohammad was born, around the year 570 CE, in the Quraysh tribe. His father died before he was born and his mother passed away when he was very young, leaving young Mohammad to be raised by Abu Talib, his uncle. He grew to be an earnest man who garnered a reputation for his skills in trade and diligence in his work. These traits greatly impressed Hazrat Khadija, a lady of means who took him into her employ. So moved by his character and ethic was Hazrat Khadija that she proposed marriage between the two, despite being many years his elder. It was to Khadija that the Prophet Mohammad first revealed the Quran at the age of forty. To her he remained faithful and singly committed till her passing, only marrying again after she had gone, despite the continuing trend among Arabians to take multiple wives.

The revelation was made to the Prophet at the fateful cave in Hira by the Archangel Gabriel. Muslims believe that from the moment of his first appearance Gabriel began to impart unto the Prophet divine revelations, which were later penned by a scribe and came to form the Holy Quran. The divine revelations compelled the Prophet to proclaim a strict monotheistic faith, departing from the prevalent "paganism" of polytheism, as well as to caution his fellow man to throw off the bonds of social injustices and evils, and prepare for the impending Day of Judgment. Initially, the Prophet's message met with growing opposition among the people of Mecca and won him only a small group of loyal followers.

Mohammad was greatly influenced by his uncle Abu Talib, and when he passed in 618, the former emigrated from the city of Mecca. He and his followers went to the city of Yathrib (which later came to be known as Medina). This migration came to be known as the Hijra, that is, the beginning of the Islamic era and the Hijra calendar.

In Medina, the Prophet became an arbitrator among the various communities of the city. While performing his duties he began to spread his message; new Quranic verses provided guidance on law and religious observance, which he used to lay the foundations of a new enlightened Islamic society. The suras revealed by the Prophet during his time in Medina also laid out his place in the long line of Biblical prophets, emphasizing the ties between the major religions of the time, the *'ahle kitab'* (People of the Book). Mohammad, being the last in this line, the teachings of Islam were seen as going beyond even those of Christianity and Judaism. After the Prophet migrated to Medina and formed an independent Muslim community, he built the first mosque with Bilal, a former slave, as the first muezzin and ordered many of his companions to recite the Quran and to learn and teach the laws that were revealed daily.

Despite its message of reform and peace, however, Islam was essentially born of revolution and conflict. War broke out between the people of Medina and the aggressor tribes of Mecca in a series of military confrontations. In the end, the Prophet secured Mecca and the allegiance of the Quraysh in 629 CE through military stratagems and political manoeuvres. The Prophet died only three years later in 632 CE. However, before his death, he managed to bring about ties with the tribal chiefs across the peninsula. Some swore allegiance to him. Others acknowledged his Prophethood and accepted the new Islamic way of life. All of these tribes gave tribute in the form of a levy towards the government set up by Mohammad, which was the foundation for the first Islamic State. Islam was, thus, in essence a rebuke of the establishment of the age and the birth of something new and progressive.

Social reforms under Islam marked a departure from the *Ayyam-i-jahiliya*, that is, the age of ignorance. In pre-Islamic Arabia, as indeed in parts of the western civilization, women were considered chattel or property of men with no right to inheritance or to own any property. The reforms introduced by Islam included the end of female infanticide prevalent in pre-Islamic Arabia, recognition of equal legal position in the law of contracts and property, as manifested in the requirement of women's consent for marriage and mehar amount as consideration, recognition of women's right to inherit/own property in their own name separate from their husbands', right to maintenance, right to seek unilateral divorce if the husband was abusive, and to remarry upon divorce or demise of husband. Many of these rights did not exist even in the West till the late nineteenth or early twentieth centuries. For instance, married women's right to own and control property was recognized by English common law only in 1882. Thus, in many ways, Islamic societies were ahead of many others in recognizing a fundamental equality of the genders.

In emphasizing the concept of equality amongst man and woman under the Shariah, I noted for the Court that even in the matter of Original Sin where Christianity holds the woman guilty, Islam lays the blame equally on both. Justice Kurian Joseph quipped that it was the snake to blame. 'We must therefore look for the snake!', I responded. The corresponding concepts in other religions like Christianity included looking at the marriage bond to be a sacred union between man and woman till death did them part. A Hindu marriage was performed by doing rounds of the sacred fire and the father did a *daan* of his daughter to the bridegroom. The bride had precious little say in the matter. Of course, subsequent legislation—the Indian Marriage Act and the Hindu Marriage Act—has changed that, but not till quite recently.

When I chose to speak on triple talaq at a university event, a feisty young lawyer who came prepared for a lively debate inevitably questioned the unilateral right of the husband to give talaq. I carefully explained that there are several other methods that gave the right to the wife as well, except that it required the intervention of a qazi or judge. (This is, of course, subject to my contention that the well-known form of talaq by the husband too requires some adjudication.) Thereafter, I thought some light-hearted repartee might be useful. Why does a Hindu bride have to follow the husband in performing the ritual of doing seven rounds of the holy fire I asked? Someone gave the young lawyer a lifeline by interjecting that the first four rounds were behind the husband but the positions were reversed for the three further rounds. This led to the question of why only three against four and why later. The point was made, though I knew that nothing really turned on it. But better still, the vice chancellor, an erudite man, told me that only four rounds are required for a complete ceremony and that three extra rounds have added by priests, perhaps to accommodate the bride.

Among the pre-Islamic Arab tribes, the right to divorce possessed by the husband was unlimited and was frequently and arbitrarily exercised without any regard to any marital obligations or responsibilities on behalf of the husband. Such social evils were well known to the Prophet Mohammad. In proclaiming the words of Allah in the Holy Quran, as well as through his teachings in his lifetime, he sought to right many of these wrongs and frame rules and laws under which the bond of matrimony would be held sacred and the position of the wife greatly elevated. Prophet Mohammad restrained the power of divorce possessed by the husbands; he gave to the women the right of obtaining separation on reasonable grounds; and towards the end of his life he went so far as practically to forbid its exercise by the men without the intervention of arbiters or a judge. He pronounced, 'talak to be the most detestable before the Almighty God of all permitted things'[7] for it prevented conjugal happiness and interfered with bringing up children properly. It is significant that the Prophet himself never divorced any of his wives and mostly married widows.

After his passing away in 632 CE, the Prophet was succeeded by four Rashidun Caliphs or the specially guided ones from amongst his companions—Hazrat Abu Bakr (632–4 CE), Hazrat Umar (634–44 CE), Hazrat Uthman (644–56 CE), and Hazrat Ali (656–61 CE), who was the Prophet's cousin and son-in-law. Although the caliphs held political authority, there was no entitlement to prophecy. Yet, any decisions taken during their stewardship, such as that of Hazrat Umar, carried greater weight than of mere heads of State.

Muslims are generally divided into two major denominations—Sunni and Shia—and their split can be traced to the death of the Prophet Mohammad. He was not just the spiritual leader of the people of the new Islamic faith, he was also the caliph of the growing Islamic community. Dispute over who would act as his successor led to three major battles—the Battle of Jamal, the Battle of Siffin, and the Battle of Karbala. It was in this final conflict that the ruling Umayyad Caliph—Yazid I—slaughtered Hussein ibn Ali and his family, leading to an outcry for revenge from Ali's supporters and an irreconcilable schism in the Islamic community. While the sting of the initial separation has long since soothed with the two communities largely living without skirmish, the divide remains. The most visible and iconic distinction is seen around Muharram, that is, the time of mourning—where both factions mourn the loss of life at that last battle, but Shias choose to relive the pain and betrayal by beating themselves upon their chests and back and drawing their own blood in commemoration of the events.

As I mentioned, the main conflict was with regard to the Prophet's successor as caliph and leader of the Islamic people. The Sunnis believed that Abu Bakr, the father of the Prophet's wife Aisha, was the rightful successor and *shura* (leaders) were meant to be elected through the procedure laid down in the Holy Quran, that is, by the consensus of the umma. On the other hand, Shias believed that the Prophet divinely ordained his cousin and son-in-law Ali Ibn Abi Talib (in accordance with the command of Allah) to be the next caliph, making Hazrat Ali and his direct descendants the true and only successors to the legacy of the Prophet. According to Shias, the Prophet's proclamation of the same is recorded in the Hadith of the Pond of Khumm. Ali Ibn Abi Talib never raised any claim to caliphate himself, and remained totally loyal to all the three caliphs elected before him. Sunnis thus follow the Rashidun (rightly guided caliphs), who were the first four caliphs who ruled after the death of the Prophet.

After the third caliph, Uthman ibn Affan, was assassinated, Ali Ibn Abi Talib was finally elected as the fourth caliph. Ali, being more concerned about restoring peace in the land, stayed back from taking any immediate action against the assassins of the previous caliph, Uthman. In the Battle of the Camel (656), Aisha opposed her stepson-in-law Ali outside the city of Basra, because she wanted justice meted to the assassins of the previous caliph, Uthman. Aisha's forces were defeated and the Prophet's widow was respectfully escorted back to Medina.

According to the Shias, Ali was the true first caliph, being so divinely selected, and they thus do not recognize the reign of the first three caliphs. They believe that Ali was the most divinely inspired and true man, second only to the Prophet Mohammad, and his descendants—the imams—are the sole legitimate Islamic leaders. The Shia Imamate thus served far more as Prophets than the Sunni caliphs. While the latter were mere men who were selected to act as leaders, the former were believed to possess divine qualities, like the Prophet. Twelver-Shias,[8] in fact, believe that the imams are immaculate from sin and human error and can understand and interpret the hidden inner meaning of the teachings of Islam. Thus the imams are trustees or holders of the light of the Prophet (Nur Muhammadin).

Considerable time was spent by counsel in establishing the sources of Shariah. Obviously, there was no difficulty in accepting that the core beliefs and precepts of Islam are to be found in the Holy Quran as revealed to the Prophet.

It might be interesting for the uninitiated to note that the Prophet of Islam was not able to read and write and, in that sense, was part of the oral literary tradition of ancient Arabia—essentially, the art of storytelling that comprised relating great epics that included didacticism. In recent times, there has been a revival of *dastangoi* in India under the intellectual leadership of S.R. Farooqi and his nephew, Mahmood Farooqui, and is being carried on by young *dastangoi*s like Ankit Chadha, but that tradition flows from Persian sources. Some people believe that Allah deliberately chose the Prophet to be unlettered or *ummi* so as not to be suspected of having himself created the details of the revelation.

The Concept of Marriage under Muslim Law

Shariah introduced the idea of marriage as a pious civil contract further enforcing the claim that Islam treats man and woman as equal. This is to be contrasted with the treatment of women in other religions, including Christianity and Hinduism. Marriage in Islam is described thus: 'No sacrament but marriage has maintained its sanctity since the earliest time. It is an act of ibadat or piety for it preserves mankind free from pollution [...] It is instituted by divine command among members of the human species.'[9] The institution of marriage is seen as an important dimension of Muslim society. The binding contract of marriage depends on offer by the man and acceptance by the woman in the presence of one advocate representative of the qazi and two witnesses representing the two sides. Although in traditional weddings the bride remains in private quarters and the witnesses carry her consent to the bridegroom and the qazi, in recent times there are increasing instances of the bride being personally present before the qazi. The bride-to-be is told that the husband-to-be has proposed for her hand for a mehar (consideration or dower). The contract of marriage or nikahnama compulsorily includes mehar for marriage to be paid to the bride immediately, though the bride often agrees to defer payment during the subsistence of the marriage; of course, it is to be paid not later than granting of a divorce, in case of such an eventuality. This was a precursor to pre-nuptial agreements familiar to contemporary developed societies and has the potential to include any wholesome condition, including the rejection of triple talaq.

An Islamic marriage may be of three kinds under Sunni law:

i. **Valid (*sahih*)**: A marriage which conforms with the legal requirements in all respects is a valid marriage.
ii. **Void (*batil*)**: A marriage contracted between parties on whom absolute prohibition applies is void. Absolute prohibitions arise from a legitimate and illegitimate relationship of blood (consanguinity), from alliance or affinity, and from fosterage.
iii. **Irregular or invalid (*fasid*)**: A marriage contracted between parties on whom relative, prohibitory, or directory prohibitions apply is voidable. Relative prohibitions arise from causes that render the marriage only invalid, for the cause that creates the bar may be removed at any time, thus rendering the union lawful ab initio without the necessity of a fresh contract. Thus, a man may not marry two sisters or a woman and her niece by the same contract or one after

> another while the previous marriage is subsisting. But if such a marriage is contracted in fact, it is invalid (fasid) but not void (*batil*), for the prior marriage may get dissolved any time by death or divorce and thus validate the second union. Prohibitive incapacity, for example, springs from the fact that the woman is already the wife of another man. A man cannot marry the widow or divorcee of another man during her iddat.

The nikah ceremony is conducted by a traditional qazi, who is a Muslim priest, though not necessarily trained in *fiqh* or Islamic jurisprudence (unlike a qazi who heads the community of priests in an area). The ceremony usually involves the qazi appointing two witnesses and a *vakil* (advocate) to seek the consent of the bride to marry the bridegroom for a stated mehar. The vakil identifies the bride, and the three report the consent to the qazi, who then confirms the marriage. A certificate is given to both sides with the signatures of the qazi, the husband, the wife, the vakil, and the two witnesses. It is significant to note that the offer of marriage with a particular mehar comes from the man to the woman and never the other way round. In this way, and many others, Muslim marriage does not strictly assign identical rights and duties to both sides. However, it is important to look at the scheme in toto and remember that equality and uniformity cannot always be equated.

The Concept of Divorce under Muslim Law

It must be understood that the dissolution of marriage has been disapproved but made permissible because of practical considerations. In this, Islam has been at the forefront of divorce law well ahead of other systems that are even now catching up. The petitions filed before the Supreme Court were primarily directed against the practice of triple talaq, described as unilateral, instantaneous, irreversible divorce in one sitting or one act of communication. In addition, there were a sprinkling of grievances about talaq by email, WhatsApp, telephone, etc. While this is examined hereafter, it is important to note that divorce in Islam is not restricted to the husband's exclusive and untrammelled right but provides several other modes that give a comparatively greater role to the woman, even equal to that of a man. Here, as noted above, the importance of the nikahnama is key as all conscionable terms may be included therein. Dr Zeenat Shaukat Ali first proposed a standard form in India in her book on Islam[10] and another draft has been approved by the Personal Law Board and needs to be widely circulated and insisted upon.

Under Muslim Law, a marriage is dissolved either by the death of a spouse or by divorce that has been properly granted. When the dissolution of the marriage tie proceeds from the husband, it is called talaq. On the face of it, this seems like the power of the husband is unilateral and absolute; but examined closely, it is restricted by the need of proper cause and in practice, it is restrained, having been limited by the requirements that govern how it is practised.

A talaq, whether oral or in writing, may of course be made without witnesses. Talaq without witnesses is said to be valid under Sunni law. Under the Shia law, a talaq is not effective unless it is pronounced strictly in accordance with the Sunnah, in Arabic terms, which means it needs to proceed in the presence of at least two adult male witnesses, with the distinct intention to dissolve the marriage tie, out of the husband's own free will, without any restraint or pressure brought to bear upon him, being sane and having sound understanding while pronouncing it and after attainment of puberty. However, the Holy Quran categorically ordains that if conditions point to a breakdown of marriage, two persons, one from each side, should attempt to reconcile the differences and resolve disputes between the parties. This inevitably brings witnesses into the picture. Failure of their efforts need to be reported to someone, perhaps the qazi, who in turn would need to ascertain the prompt payment of mehar, proper arrangement for residence of the wife during the iddat period, and provision for the divorced woman for that period and for the children till they reach puberty. This can only be done by a person in authority, such as the qazi. Since the office of the qazi has since fallen into disuse, it is the Family Court that could handle this but somehow that does not seem to have happened. This also explains why it is found necessary for the woman to seek assistance from court while the man appears to be able to call the shots himself. However, although he might have the power to pronounce talaq on his own, this makes clear that the qazi still has a role and it is the absence of one that is creating all the problems. In fact, a section of jurists, consisting mainly of *Mu'tazilas*, emphasize upon the requirement of the sanction of qazi, without which talaq is not permissible. They derive support from the Prophet's words, stating that talaq is the most detestable of all permitted things, as well as from the requirement of arbiters in case of a dispute. Therefore, according to these jurists, talaq should be tested by an unbiased judge to ensure that it is exercised within the permitted limits.

When a definite and complete separation (*talaq-ul-bain*) has taken place, the parties so separated cannot remarry without the formality of the woman marrying another man and being divorced from him (*halala*). This rule was framed with the object of restraining the frequency of divorce in Arabia.

Every woman married to a man by a lawful contract is bound, for the prevention of confusion of parentage, to observe probation in the case of the dissolution of the marriage tie. But if the marriage is invalid and the parties have separated before actual consummation, there is no requirement of observing iddat. But if consummation has taken place, the iddat will be reckoned from the time of separation (*tafriq*).

A talaq may be effected by the husband, and at times by the wife, in many of forms, though generally the most known or prescribed modes are one of four: (i) Talaq-ul-sunnat, (ii) Ila, (iii) Zihar, and (iv) Talaq-ul-bidat. Many other forms exist, and are effected, but are lesser known. A brief description of these lesser and better known forms is here below:

i. **Talaq-ul-sunnat:** This is a divorce that is effected in accordance with the rules laid down in the traditions (the *Sunnah*) handed down from the Prophet or his principal disciples. It is, in fact, the mode or procedure that seems to have been approved of by him at the beginning of his ministry, and is, consequently, regarded as the regular or proper form of divorce. It can be further sub-divided into:

a. **Ahsan:** In Arabic, the word means 'best' or 'very proper'. In this form of the *talaq-ul-sunnat*, the husband is required to submit to the following conditions: (1) he must pronounce the formula of divorce once, in a single sentence; (2) he must do so when the woman is in a state of purity (*tuhr*); and (3) he must abstain from conjugal rights after pronouncing the formula for three *tuhr*s (iddat period). The last clause is intended to demonstrate that the resolve on the husband's part to separate from the wife is not a passing whim, but is the result of a settled determination. Thus, clearly iddat serves two purposes: to confirm if there is a child in the mother's womb and to impose additional responsibilities on the father, in addition to providing time to cool off or rethink and revoke the pronouncement of divorce before it becomes irrevocable. In case the woman is found to be bearing a child, the iddat and all its consequences are extended to nine months or till childbirth.

For this reason, in the *ahsan* form, divorce is revocable during the iddat period. The revocation may be either express or implied. An example of implied revocation would be where the husband and wife start cohabiting with each other before the conclusion of the iddat period. On the lapse of the term of three tuhrs or the iddat period, the separation takes effect as an irrevocable divorce but the couple is free to reunite by a fresh nikah.

b. **Hasan:** In Arabic, the word 'hasan' means 'good' or 'proper'. In this form, the husband pronounces the formula thrice, once each during three successive tuhrs. The talaq becomes irrevocable once the last or third pronouncement is made and no fresh nikah is permissible between the couple unless there has been an intervening marriage of the woman to another man.

ii. **Talaq-e-Tafweez**: This is the delegation by the man of his right to the woman or further delegating it to an agent even while retaining it to himself. This can be written into the nikahnama as indeed any other term such as no triple talaq. An agreement can also be made to the effect any time after the marriage ceremony (as a sort of post-nuptial agreement). The courts have upheld the validity of such a divorce in cases such as *Mohd. Amin v. Mst. Aimna Bibi* and *Aziz v. Mt. Naro*. Talaq-e-tafweez may be of three kinds: (a) *ikhtiar*, giving the wife authority to talaq herself. The delegation may be subject to certain conditions, such as if the wife is not maintained properly, etc., (b) *amr-ba-yed*, leaving the matter in her hand, and (c) *mashiat*, giving her the option to do what she likes at her will.

iii. **Ila:** When the husband refrains from sexual intercourse with his wife for a period of four months or more pursuant to a vow, it constitutes divorce by way of ila.

iv. **Zihar:** If the husband likens his wife to his mother or any other female within prohibited degrees, the wife has a right to ask the husband to do penance and refuse herself to him till he has done so. If the husband refuses to do penance or does not do it properly, the wife is entitled to a judicial divorce on such ground. This form of divorce is called *zihar*.

v. **Khula:** A divorce by *khula* is a divorce initiated by the wife in lieu of a consideration to the husband.

The terms of the bargain are matters of arrangement between the husband and wife, but the husband has no right to refuse the dissolution. The observance of iddat is still necessary, even though the divorce becomes irrevocable as soon as the consideration is accepted by the husband.

vi. **Lian:** A woman is entitled to divorce on the grounds that her husband has falsely charged her with adultery.

vii. **Mubarat:** A *mubarat* divorce is like divorce by mutual consent prevalent under other laws. Under this form, the husband and wife may obtain divorce when both of them agree to separate from each other. The wife has a right to give an offer of divorce to the husband and vice versa. Once the offer is accepted by the other spouse, the divorce becomes irrevocable. However, as in the case of khula, iddat needs to be necessarily observed.

viii. **Fasq:** *Fasq* allows the wife to get the marriage annulled with the help of a qazi even if the husband is against it. The woman opting for it has to publicize her plan to seek divorce, and most women give '*fasq*' ads in newspapers. Theoretically, this form of divorce (or rather annulment) is available to either party on grounds that overlap with khula for the woman (or as under the Dissolution of Muslim Marriages Act, 1939). The Hanafi law, however, does not recognize *fasq* as a mode of dissolution of marriage. That is precisely the reason why the Dissolution of Muslim Marriages Act, 1939 (hereinafter, 1939 Act) was enacted in order to 'consolidate and clarify the provisions of Muslim law' and recognize *fasq* (judicial divorce), which was already a part of the Muslim Personal Law (Shariah).

The following Statement of Objects and Reasons of the 1939 Act is noteworthy in this regard:

> There is no proviso in the Hanafi Code of Muslim Law enabling a married Muslim woman to obtain a decree from the court dissolving her marriage in case the husband neglects to maintain her, makes her life miserable by deserting or persistently maltreating her or absconds leaving her unprovided for and under certain other circumstances. The absence of such a provision has entailed unspeakable misery to innumerable Muslim women in British India. The Hanafi Jurists, however, have clearly laid down that in cases in which the application of Hanafi Law causes hardship, it is permissible to apply the provisions of the Maliki, Shafi'i or Hambali Law.

This is a clear example of harmonizing of different schools of Islamic jurisprudence, which was also undertaken under the Shariat (Shariah) Application Act, 1937, giving precedence to Shariah over local customs and usages. In order to apply the Shariah, not only had the courts to wean out custom and usage, but also to find common ground between the four schools. That indeed is the exercise this Court has to undertake in the instant case.

ix. **Talaq-ul-bidat:** The glossary of Islamic terms in the English translation of *Sahih Muslim* translated by Nasiruddin al-Khattab, gives the following definition of *bid'ah*:

> *Bid'ah*: Any heresy or innovated practice introduced in the religion of Allah which have no basis in the Qur'ân or Sunnah and to regard these new things as acts of Ibâdah. The Prophet said that every Bid'ah is a deviation from the true path and every deviation leads to Hell-fire.[11]

As the name signifies, *talaq-ul-bidat* is a form of talaq based on innovation, introduced during the second century of the Mohammedan era. When a husband pronounces talaq three times during one single tuhr either in one sentence, 'I divorce you thrice', or in separate sentences, 'I divorce you, I divorce you, I divorce you', or, a single pronouncement made during a *tuhr* clearly indicating an intention to irrevocably dissolve the marriage, 'I divorce you irrevocably', it constitutes *talaq-ul-bidat*. The Privy Council described it as bad in theology, good in law. Interestingly, the Muslim Personal Law Board also subscribed to this thesis before the Supreme Court and insisted that this has been the accepted practice for 1,400 years. Curiously, no empirical data was provided and a recent survey of 30,000 divorce cases amongst Muslim women submitted to the Court by the Board shows less than 1 per cent cases of triple talaq, used by the Board to insist that the practice was a dying one and did not require the Court's intervention!

Having said that, it must be understood that the concept of *talaq-ul-bidat* or irregular talaq itself is based on the limit of three talaqs placed on the man, that is, that he can divorce his wife only three times in life, the first two being revocable within the iddat and the third being final and irrevocable. Furthermore, even if the first two are not revoked during the iddat period, they can yet be followed by fresh nikah, but that option is not available after the third. In the remote chance of the couple wishing to marry again, it is possible only if the woman has been married to another man and divorced, known as *halala*. This restriction was placed to ensure that talaq did not become a whimsical mockery. Sadly, however, this limit of three divorces and the ultimate concession for an unfortunate woman whose marriage to another man also ends, has been twisted to appear an evil and thoughtless condition of humiliation imposed on the woman. The truth is that such a situation is accepted only if it happens in the normal course and any engineered or contrived situation is not accepted by Shariah.

It is important that the entire marriage and divorce arrangement be seen in its entirety to judge its reasonableness. Thus, the restricted unilateral power of talaq granted to the man needs to be considered in the context of marriage where it is the man who brings a proposal of marriage for a consideration of mehar and the woman who has to accept it. There is no provision for a similar proposal made by the woman for the acceptance of the man. Therefore, in judging the man–woman relationship in Islam, particularly for divorce, one has to keep in mind that equality does not mean uniformity.

ix. **Talaq-ul-bain:** When a definite and complete separation (*talaq-ul-bain*) has taken place, the parties so separated cannot remarry without the formality of the woman marrying another man and being divorced from him (*halala*). This rule was framed with the object of restraining the frequency of divorce in Arabia.

Here it is important to make clear one more concept, that is, iddat (probation). Every woman married to a man by a lawful contract is bound, for the prevention of confusion of parentage, to observe probation in the case of the dissolution of the marriage tie. But if the marriage is invalid and the parties have separated before actual consummation, there is no requirement of observing iddat.

But if consummation has taken place, the iddat will be reckoned from the time of separation (tafriq).

It is believed, and the Attorney General very forcefully argued, that talaq in any form is unilateral, the monopoly of the man, and extrajudicial. It, therefore, ex-facie violates Article 14 of the Constitution and is void. He pleaded with the Court to quash all forms of talaq and undertook to have legislation done to replace it with a statutory form of divorce for Muslims. However, the Attorney General avoided admitting to the Court that this is but a small part of divorce in Shariah. To begin with, talaq pronounced by the husband has to be for a good cause and must be preceded by attempts at reconciliation by two persons—one from the husband's family and another from the wife's. This view has been upheld by the Guwahati High Court, a Full Bench of the Bombay High Court, and the Kerala High Court in *Musstt. Rebun Nessa v. Musstt. Bibi Ayesha,*[12] *Dagdu Chotu Pathan v. Rahimbi Dagdu Pathan & Ors.*[13]*, and A. Yousuf Rawther v. Sowramma,*[14] respectively.

Mere pronouncement of Talaq by the husband or merely declaring his intentions or is acts of having pronounced the Talaq is not sufficient and does not meet the requirements of law. All the stages of conveying the reasons for divorce, appointment of arbiters, the arbiters resorting to conciliation proceedings so as to bring reconciliation between the parties and the failure of such proceedings or a situation where it was impossible for the marriage to continue, are required to be proved as conditions precedent for the husband's right to give Talaq to his wife. It is, thus, not merely the factum of Talaq but the conditions preceding to this stage of giving Talaq are also required to be proved when the wife disputes the factum of Talaq or the effectiveness of Talaq or the legality of Talaq before a court of law. Mere statement made in writing before the court, in any form, or in oral depositions regarding the Talaq having been pronounced sometimes in the past is not sufficient to hold that the husband has divorced his wife.

As Syed Ameer Ali quotes from *Radd-ul-Muhtar*, 'Talaq is permitted only when the wife by her conduct or her words does injury to the husband or happens to be impious.... And it is *wajib* (obligatory) when the husband cannot fulfil his duties, as when he is impotent or an eunuch.'[15] Talaq is permitted only when there is a necessity of release from the marital tie. Therefore, if there is no reasonable cause for a talaq, which would render it *mubah* (permissible/permitted), it is not valid.

Although the Attorney General would have wanted a wide canvas, he sought to cut losses by resting his case upon an endorsement of the Delhi High Court judgment of Justice Badar Ahmed. Of the judgments from Guwahati, Kerala, Madras and Delhi, it was only the last one that analysed triple talaq in detail and on the facts required to do so, while all the other judgments were read to be obiter, as on the facts, the issue did not arise.

In questioning talaq as being unilateral and extrajudicial, the Attorney General and some other counsels contrasted the position of the man with that of the woman, who is required to approach a court of law under the Dissolution of Muslim Marriages Act, 1939. Furthermore, while the woman could seek divorce only on the grounds enumerated therein (though pretty comprehensive by any standard), a man had no such conditions to bind him (but that is also not the true and correct view of Shariah). This must however, to some extent, be seen and considered in practical terms. A man, in seeking divorce, has no further relief to seek while the woman needs to get her mehar if not already paid, proper accommodation for the iddat period, maintenance, and provision for herself and children. Thus the situation is already one where there the two parties are not equal, sometimes to the prejudice of the man. The system of divorce under Shariah thus makes distinctions, while trying wholistically to attain some form of equality.

Furthermore, besides talaq as described, there are other methods by which a marriage can be brought to an end, including what is called dissolution or annulment, the effect in either case being the same. In other words, the impression that talaq or divorce in Shariah is unilateral and extrajudicial is erroneous.

Sources of Muslim Law

The basic source of Muslim law is divine revelation: one is the direct word of Allah—the Holy Quran—and the other is the indirect word of God—the Sunnah. These two forms of revelations are said to be the root of Islamic law.

The Holy Quran

Prophet Mohammad (Muḥammad ibn ʿAbdullāh ibn ʿAbdul-Muṭṭalib ibn Hāshim) is considered by Muslims to be the last Messenger and Prophet of Allah, sent to guide humanity towards the path of righteousness and good. Thus to him was revealed the central text of the faith—the Holy Quran—whose words were meant to guide the Prophet in restoring the original monotheistic faith that was propagated before Mohammad by Adam, Ibrahim (Abraham), Musa (Moses), 'Isa (Jesus), and others. The Holy Quran thus speaks familiarly of many major narratives from the other biblical scriptures; while it touches on some summarily, it speaks at length of others, sometimes offering an alternative account of events. At times, the Book gives great detail about historical events and often looks to find the moral significance of events. The moral, cultural, spiritual, and other teachings of the books as they were revealed to Mohammad became the foundation of the Islamic faith.

It is believed that the words of the Holy Quran were revealed gradually over a period of approximately 23 years, beginning on 22 December 609 CE (when the Prophet was forty) and concluding in 632, the year of his death. According to the traditional narrative, several companions of Mohammad served as scribes and were responsible for writing down the revelations. It is one such event that has been debated amongst scholars of Islam and used as the backdrop of the controversial *Satanic Verses* by Salman Rushdie. Shortly after the Prophet's death, the Quran was compiled by his companions who wrote down and memorized parts of it. These codices had differences that motivated Caliph Uthman to establish a standard version now known as Uthman's codex, which is generally considered the archetype of the Holy Quran known today.

The Holy Quran is thus the word of Allah revealed to his Messenger and last Prophet upon Earth. It is said that the Archangel Gabriel first appeared to the Prophet in a secluded cave in Hira. Upon seeing the vision of the Angel's presence the Prophet broke into a sweat, not knowing what to make of the revelation. However, as he came to understand the purpose of the visitation, he repeated after Gabriel the words now enshrined in the Sura 'Alaq (The Clot):[16]

Read (Proclaim) In the name of Name of your Lord who created
Created man, out of a clot (of congealed blood)
Read (Proclaim), and your Lord is the Most Generous
who taught by the Pen,
Taught man that which he knew not

Mohammad's first revelation, according to the Quran, was accompanied with a vision. The agent of revelation is mentioned as the 'one mighty in power', the one who 'grew clear to view when he was on the uppermost horizon. Then he drew nigh and came down till he was (distant) two bows' length or even nearer.' The Islamic studies scholar Alford T. Welch states in the *Encyclopaedia of Islam* that he believes the graphic descriptions of Mohammad's condition at these moments may be regarded as genuine, because he was severely disturbed after these revelations. According to Welch, these seizures would have been seen by those around him as convincing evidence for the superhuman origin of Mohammad's inspirations.

From then on, the Prophet would memorize the words that Gabriel would say unto him and repeat it to the *sahaba* (his followers)—beginning, after the occasion of the first revelation, with his wife Hazrat Khadija. The *sahaba* would then write it down for posterity on pieces of leather, bark, or bone. Interestingly, the Quran describes the Prophet as *'ummi'*, which is traditionally interpreted as illiterate. However, medieval commentators such as Muhammad ibn Jarir al-Tabari (d. 923 CE) maintained that the term induced two meanings: first, the inability to read or write in general; second, inexperience or ignorance of the previous books or scriptures. Mohammad's illiteracy was thus taken as a sign of the genuineness of his Prophethood. For example, according to Fakhr al-Din al-Razi, if Mohammad had mastered writing and reading he possibly would have been suspected of having studied the books of the ancestors. His being unable to read or write thus meant that the teachings he sought to relay had indeed been imparted unto him by some divine source.

Even though the people of Mecca trusted Mohammad greatly, the task of relaying the revelation would be a difficult one. It is said that Mohammad thus gathered people together and first asked them if they would believe him if he told them a great army was gathering just beyond a nearby hill. The people replied that they would believe anything he said, as he was an honest and trustworthy man. The Prophet then told the people of the words relayed to him by Gabriel, of the message of Allah. And so Islam was born.

The Holy Quran, as it exists today, was not the order in which it was revealed to the Prophet Mohammad. Often the suras were revealed in light of situations that presented themselves. The suras thus deal with a vast array of topics and themes—from moral values and social obligations to law and politics. There were also times when people came directly to the Prophet for advice and guidance. The advice, when given, as well as his actions towards others and his observances in life, were also passed on or written down—primarily by his companions, but sometimes by others who bore witness. The passing of these teachings orally came to be the Sunnah and when written, they became the Hadith. Thus, being the descriptions of the truest believer and most faithful amongst men, the Hadith became an additional source of Shariah with *Sahih Bukhari* and *Sahih Muslim* being the main, most relied upon.

The word *qur'ān* appears about seventy times in the Quran itself, assuming various meanings. It is the noun form of the Arabic verb *qara'a*, meaning 'he read' or 'he recited'. While some Western scholars consider the word to be derived from the Syriac, the majority of Muslim authorities hold the origin of the word is *qara'a* itself. An important meaning of the word is the 'act of reciting', as reflected in an early Quranic passage: 'It is for Us to collect it and to recite it (qur'ānahu).'

There are in all 114 suras or chapters of the Quran of unequal length, the shortest chapter ('Al-Kawthar') has only three *aiyat* (verses) while the longest ('Al-Baqara') contains 286. Of the 114 chapters in the Qur'an, 87 are classified as Meccan, while 27 are Medinan.

The term also has closely related synonyms that are employed throughout the Quran. Each synonym possesses its own distinct meaning, but its use may converge with that of *qur'ān* in certain contexts. Such terms include *kitāb* (book); *āyah* (sign); and *sūrah* (scripture). The latter two also denote units of revelation. In the large majority of contexts, usually with a definite article (*al-*), the word is referred to as the 'revelation' (*waḥy*), that which has been 'sent down' (*tanzīl*) at intervals. Other related words are: *dhikr* (remembrance), used to refer to the Quran in the sense of a reminder and warning, and *ḥikmah* (wisdom), sometimes referring to the revelation or part of it.

The Quran describes itself as 'the discernment' (*al-furqān*), 'the mother book' (*umm al-kitāb*), 'the guide' (*huda*), 'the wisdom' (*hikmah*), 'the remembrance' (*dhikr*), and 'the revelation' (*tanzīl*; something sent down, signifying the descent of an object from a higher place to lower place). Another term is *al-kitāb* (the book), though it is also used in Arabic for other scriptures, such as the Torah and the Gospels. The term *mus'haf* ('written work') is often used to refer to particular Quranic manuscripts but is also used in the Quran to identify earlier revealed books. It is important to keep in mind that classical Arabic has a rich vocabulary with each word subject to several meanings. Therefore, seeking the inner or deeper meaning of the text of the Quran is a challenge.

On the 9th of Dhil-Hajj of 10 AH,[17] the Prophet gave a historic speech in the plain of Arafat in which he summed up the main points of his teachings. The Prophet first thanked God for His countless mercies and blessings, and then said:[18]

O Muslims! Listen to me with attention. This may be the last occasion when I am with you, and I may not be alive to perform another Hajj.

God is One and He has no partners. Do not associate anyone or anything with Him. Worship Him, fear Him, obey Him and love Him. Do not miss your mandatory prayers. Observe faithfully the month of fasting. Pay Zakat (poor-tax) regularly, and visit the House of God whenever you can.

Remember that everyone of you is answerable to God for everything you do on this earth, and very soon you will find yourselves in His presence.

I am abolishing all the customs, practices and traditions of the Times of Ignorance. I disclaim the right of retaliation for the blood of my cousin, Ibn Rabi'a; and I disclaim the interest on the loans given by my uncle, Abbas ibn Abdul Muttalib.

I call upon you all to show respect to the honor, life and property of each other in the same manner as you show respect to the sanctity of this day. All believers are brothers of each other. If something belongs to any one of them, it is unlawful for others to take it without his permission.

Be sincere in your words and deeds, and be sincere to each other, and remain united at all times.

You have rights in regard to women; so also you have duties toward them. Treat them with love, kindness, respect and affection.

The slaves you own were also created by God. Do not be cruel to them. If they err, forgive them. Give them to eat what you eat and give them to wear the same kind of clothes as you wear.

The members of my family are like the pole-star. They will lead to salvation all those who will obey them and follow them. I leave among you a composite heritage—the Book of God (Qur'an) and the members of my family. Both of them are complementary to each other and are inseparable from each other. If you defer to both of them you will never go astray.

And remember that I am the last of the Messengers of God to mankind. After me there will be no other messenger or messengers of God.

This should be an eye-opener for persons who dwell upon what they think are unacceptably arcane and regressive postures of Islam. Coming straight from the Prophet in his farewell sermon, such directives—of foregoing retaliation for the blood of a cousin, disclaiming interest on loans, speaking of women in terms of rights and duties, love and respect due to them, and of course, speaking of slaves as creatures of God to be fed and clothed as oneself—cannot but be the loadstone for the true understanding of Islam.

The Prophet of Islam is considered by Muslims to be the personification of perfection in human character. Believers strive to live their lives according to the *sira* (character) of the Prophet and his Sunnah. They believe that God willed that not the slightest blemish come on his character; thus, despite the many battles he participated in, there is no record of any fatality caused by him personally. Many Muslims try to live their lives consistent with their understanding of the Prophet's life. Those, for instance, who believe that he had long flowing locks let their own hair grow, but there are others who believe that he trimmed his hair short, and hence follow that practice. Generally, mullahs wear their hair short and persons associated with Sufi thinking have flowing locks.

The Prophet applied the principles and precepts stated in the Holy Quran to facts in practice. Consequently, what was said, done, or agreed to by the Prophet became another immutable primary source of Muslim law. The narrations of what was said, done, or agreed to by Prophet are called Hadith or traditions. Of the several Hadith, it is widely accepted that some like *Sahih Bukhari* are considered more reliable than others. The only room for the exercise of human reason is within their understanding.

Amongst Sunnis, the six most authentic collections of Hadith by the six famous imams are together called Sihah Sitta or 'the authentic six' (Curiously, all these six compilers were Persian).

First among them is Muhammad bin Ismail al-Bukhari, the author of *Sahih Bukhari*. He was born in 195 AH (810 CE) at Bukhara in Central Asia and died in 256 AH (870 CE) at a place known as Khartank, near Samarkand, Uzbekistan.

Next among them is Muslim bin Hajjaj al-Nishapuri who was born in Nishapur in Iran, in 206 AH (821 CE) and died in the same city in 261 AH (874 CE). His *Sahih Muslim* is second in authenticity, next to that of Bukhari.

Abu Dawood, Sulaiman bin al-Ash'ath bin Ishaq al-Azdi as-Sijistani, who was one of the eminent imams of Hadeeth, was born in 202 AH (807 CE). He was Persian, but of Arab descent. He died at Basra on Friday in the month of Shawwal in 275 AH (888–9 CE).

Imam Tirmidhi was born in the year 209 AH (824 CE), during the reign of the Abbasid Khalifa Mamoon al Rasheed. He died in the year 279 AH (892 CE) in a village called Bugh in Uzbekistan at the ripe age of seventy.

Fifth in line of these compilers is Abu Abd al-Rahman Ahmad ibn Shu'ayb al-Nasa'i. He was born in Nasa in the Nishapur region in 215 AH (830 CE). He died in Mecca and was buried in a place between the Safa and Marwah. The year of his death was 303 AH (915 CE).

Sixth of the compilers is Abu Abdullah Muhammad ibn Yazid ibn Majah al-Rab'i al-Qazwini, commonly known as Imam Ibn Majah, was born in Qazwin in Persia in 209 AH (824 CE). He was a hafiz of *hadith* and the author of *Kitab as-Sunnah*, one of the six most authentic collections of *ahadith*. He died on 22 Ramadan 273 AH (887 CE) in Qazwin. He is the author of a famous collection of Hadith, *Sunan Ibn Majah*.

For Shias the Hadith collections comprise four books—*Kitab al-Kafi, Man la yahduruhu al-Faqih, Tandhib al-Ahkam*, and *Al-Istibar*.

Ijma and Ijtihad

Ijma and *Ijtihad* are the secondary and dependent sources. They derive their value from the primary sources. *Ijma* has been defined as the consensus of the *mujtahid*s or jurists of a certain period on a particular matter. Some people consider only those propositions as ijma as were indisputably accepted under the first four rightly directed caliphs or in the time of the companions and of the generation immediately succeeding them. Ijtihad is the process of making an independent interpretation of the legal sources, the Holy Quran, and the Sunnah by the mujtahids. As Shah Wali-Allah states, the object of ijtihad is to exert to know what would have been the judgment of the Prophet if the problem had occurred before him.[19] According to tradition, its starting point is the absence of any clearly applicable text and it may operate only so far as the judgment does not contravene the Holy Quran and the Sunnah. Ijtihad is of three kinds: *ijtihad bayani*—interpretation by way of explanation of matters expressly dealt with in the Holy Quran or Hadith but which need further elaboration; *ijtihad qiya*s—interpretation by way of analogical reasoning of matters not expressly dealt with in the two primary sources but similar to those expressly mentioned in them; and *ijtihad istislahi*—matters not expressly stated in the Holy Quran or Hadith which cannot be solved by analogical reasoning and for which *maslahah* (utilities) is considered to be the basis for arriving at a decision.

King Fahd of Saudi Arabia, in an address to a congress of theologians in Mecca in 1983, noted that the gates of ijtihad have not closed. More recently, in 2013, King

Abdullah bin Abdulaziz Al Saud too repeated the same in a statement to leaders, key Islamic personalities, and heads of Haj missions. Thus a vast opportunity continues to exist provided we approach modern-day problems with sincerity and faith.

Schools of Islamic Jurisprudence

Unlike in secular systems wherein the State has the authority to create law and to make authoritative interpretations, under the Islamic legal system, it was the jurists who had the authority to interpret the basic texts, the accepted rule of recognition of any law being that it had to be one given by God through His revealed sources, namely, the Holy Quran and the Sunnah. Thus, now the accepted rule of recognition of any law came to be that it must be derived from the sources by jurists in accordance with the principles of jurisprudence (*usul-al-fiqh*). Beyond the treatises of the maslaqs, and as part of it, is the process of ijma or consensus amongst scholars, qiyas or ijtihad, or analytical endeavours of scholars. The absence of any central authority to decide on the correctness of an interpretation meant that different interpretations could be made of the same text. Eventually, the study and interpretation of the Holy Quran and the Hadith and forming opinion on them, known as *fiqh*, led to the establishment of four major Sunni Schools of Islamic Jurisprudence, known as maslaq, each named after the imam who founded it. The Shia schools grew separately. With the passage of time, adhering to a school became mandatory and while ijtihad became increasingly restricted, the rule of *taqlid* (precedent) was to be followed. Thus, though a certain kind of homogeneity could be found within a specific school, Shariah continued with its pluralistic approach by accommodating different conflicting opinions of the schools. It is this pluralistic character of the Islamic system which sometimes enabled picking and choosing the opinion of one school over the other.

Procedure of Talaq as per the Sources of Muslim Law

Marriage in its essence is an act of chastity established by the law [per se] not admitting of dissolution; in order therefore, to remove the tie, it is necessary to adhere strictly to the formula prescribed for the purpose.[20]

In light of the above verse, it is important to determine the procedure prescribed for the purpose of talaq under different sources of Muslim law.

Procedure of Talaq as per the Holy Quran

Undoubtedly, the Holy Quran has nowhere ordained that three divorces pronounced in a single breath, at once will have the effect of three separate divorces. To this effect, relevant verses of the Quran can be relied upon:

i. For those who take an oath for abstention from their wives, a waiting for four months is ordained; if then they return, Allah is Oft-forgiving, Most Merciful. (2:226)
ii. But if their intention is firm for divorce, Allah heareth and knoweth all things. (2:227)
iii. Divorced women shall wait concerning themselves for three monthly periods. Nor is it lawful for them to hide what Allah Hath created in their wombs, if they have faith

in Allah and the Last Day. And their husbands have the better right to take them back in that period, if they wish for reconciliation. And women shall have rights similar to the rights against them, according to what is equitable; but men have a degree [of advantage] over them. And Allah is Exalted in Power, Wise. (2:228)

iv. A divorce is only permissible twice: after that, the parties should either hold together on equitable terms, or separate with kindness. It is not lawful for you, [Men], to take back any of your gifts [from your wives], except when both parties fear that they would be unable to keep the limits ordained by Allah. If ye [judges] do indeed fear that they would be unable to keep the limits ordained by Allah, there is no blame on either of them if she give something for her freedom. These are the limits ordained by Allah; so do not transgress them if any do transgress the limits ordained by Allah, such persons wrong [Themselves as well as others]. (2:229)

v. When ye divorce women, and they fulfil the term of their ['iddat], either take them back on equitable terms or set them free on equitable terms; but do not take them back to injure them, [or] to take undue advantage; if any one does that; He wrongs his own soul. Do not treat Allah's Signs as a jest, but solemnly rehearse Allah's favours on you, and the fact that He sent down to you the Book and Wisdom, for your instruction. And fear Allah, and know that Allah is well acquainted with all things. (2:231)

vi. If ye fear a breach between them twain, appoint [two] arbiters, one from his family and the other from hers; if they wish for peace, Allah will cause their reconciliation: For Allah hath full knowledge, and is acquainted with all things. (4:35)

vii. O ye who believe! When ye marry believing women, and then divorce them before ye have touched them, no period of 'Iddat have ye to count in respect of them: so give them a present. And set them free in a handsome manner. (33:49)

viii. O Prophet! When ye do divorce women, divorce them at their prescribed periods, and count [accurately], their prescribed periods: And fear Allah your Lord: and turn them not out of their houses, nor shall they [themselves] leave, except in case they are guilty of some open lewdness, those are limits set by Allah: and any who transgresses the limits of Allah, does verily wrong his [own] soul: thou knowest not if perchance Allah will bring about thereafter some new situation. (65:1)

ix. Thus when they fulfil their term appointed, either take them back on equitable terms or part with them on equitable terms; and take for witness two persons from among you, endued with justice, and establish the evidence [as] before Allah. Such is the admonition given to him who believes in Allah and the Last Day. And for those who fear Allah, He [ever] prepares a way out. (65:2)

x. Such of your women as have passed the age of monthly courses, for them the prescribed period, if ye have any doubts, is three months, and for those who have no courses [it is the same]: for those who carry [life within their wombs], their period is until they deliver their burdens: and for those who fear Allah, He will make their path easy. (65:4)

Therefore, according to the Holy Quran, divorce is permissible only twice during the lifetime of the husband. The possibility of being with the wife is still open after two pronouncements of divorce. It is only after the third divorce is pronounced that the divorce becomes irrevocable. The essence of the provision is to give some time to the husband to make a conscious decision as to whether he wants to irrevocably break the marriage tie and also to stop the earlier practice of divorcing the wife as many times as one may wish for during their lifetime.

Validity of Triple Talaq as per the Sunnah

Bid'ah, as we have already seen, is a form of innovation and is not covered under the procedure established by the Holy Quran. There is yet another kind of innovation talked about in Islam: *zindiq*.

Zindiq: One who goes so far into innovated and deviant beliefs and philosophizing, etc., without sticking to the truth found in the Qur'ân and the Sunnah to such an extreme extent that they actually leave Islam altogether.[21]

Now, the question arises whether such forms of innovations, or indeed triple talaq, are valid under the Sunnah. The fact that mere repetition of divorce thrice in one sitting does not amount to a *mughallaza* or final divorce finds support in the following traditions from *Sahih Muslim*:[22]

i. **[3652] 1 – (1471)** It was narrated from Ibn 'Umar that he divorced his wife while she was menstruating, at the time of the Messenger of Allâh. 'Umar bin Al-Khattâb asked the Messenger of Allâh about that and the Messenger of Allâh said to him: "Tell him to take her back, then wait until she has become pure, then menstruated again, then become pure again. Then if he wishes he may keep her, or if he wishes he may divorce her before he has intercourse with her. That is the *'Iddah* (prescribed periods) for which Allâh has enjoined the divorce of women."

ii. **[3673] 15 – (1472)** It was narrated that Ibn 'Abbâs said: "During the time of the Messenger of Allâh it, Abû Bakr and the first two years of 'Umar's Khilâfah, a threefold divorce was counted as one. Then 'Umar bin Al-Khattâb said: 'People have become hasty in a matter in which they should take their time. I am thinking of holding them to it.' So he made it binding upon them."

iii. **[3674] 16 – (...)** Ibn Tawûs narrated from his father that Abû As-Sahbâ' said to Ibn 'Abbâs: "Do you know that the threefold divorce was regarded as one at the time of the Messenger of Allâh and Abû Bakr, and for three years of 'Umar's leadership?" He said: "Yes."

iv. **[3675] 17 – (...)** It was narrated from Tawûs that Abû As-Sahbâ' said to Ibn 'Abbâs: "Tell us of something interesting that you know. Wasn't the threefold divorce counted as one at the time of the Messenger of Allâh and Abû Bakr?" He said: "That was so, then at the time of 'Umar the people began to issue divorces frequently, so he made it binding upon them."

v. **[2005] 43 – (867)** It was narrated that Jâbir bin 'Abdullâh said: "When the Messenger of Allâh delivered a *Khutbah*, his eyes would turn red, his voice would become loud, and his anger would increase, until it was as if he was warning of an attacking army, saying: 'The enemy will attack in the morning or in the evening.' He said: 'The Hour and I have been sent like these two,' and he held his index finger and middle finger up together. And he would say: 'The best of speech is the Book of Allâh, the best of guidance is the guidance of Muhammad, and the worst of matters are those which are newly-invented, and every innovation is a going astray.' Then he would say: 'I am closer to every believer than his own self. Whoever leaves behind wealth, it is for his family; whoever leaves behind a debt or dependents, then the responsibility of paying it off and of caring for them rests upon me.'"

vi. **[4796] 59 – (1852)** It was narrated that Ziyâd bin 'Ilâqah said: "I heard 'Arfajah say: 'I heard the Messenger of Allâh say: "There will be Fitnah and innovations. Whoever wants to divide this *Ummah* when it is united, strike him with the sword, no matter who he is."'"

vii. **[4797] (...)** A similar report (as no. 2796) was narrated from 'Arfajah from the Prophet, except that in their Hadîth it says: "... kill him".

In addition, author Aqil Ahmad offers following accounts of traditions[23]:

i. "Mahmud-b, Labeed reported that the Messenger of Allah was informed about a man who gave three divorces at a time to his wife. Then he got up enraged and said; Are you playing with the Book of Allah who is great and glorious while I am still amongst you? So much so that a man got up and said; shall I not kill him."

ii. There is another tradition reported by Rokanah-b. Abu Yazid that he gave his wife Sahalmash an irrevocable divorce, and he conveyed it to the Messenger of Allah and Said; by Allah, I have not intended but one divorce. Then the Messenger of Allah asked Have you not intended but one (Divorce)? Rokana said; By Allah, I did not intend but one divorce. The Messenger of Allah then returned her back to him. Afterwards he divorced her for second time at the time of Hadrat Omar and [the] third time at the time of Hadrat Osman.

iii. During Caliph Omar's time when people started misusing the facility and indulged in widespread triple divorce, reverting back to the wife after swearing to their intention of giving a single divorce, Caliph, Hadrat Umar decreed that triple divorce would become effective, refusing to allow the couple to revert to each other since the facility of oath taking had been turned into a meaningless game by many.

As ordained by the Holy Quran, the acts and sayings of Prophet are to be obeyed. Therefore, when we have the Hadith stating in clear terms that Prophet considered three divorces in one sitting as one, the deeds of the companions need not be seen; it would not be proper to do so. It is reported that once, when news was brought to him that one of his disciples had divorced his wife, pronouncing the three talaqs at one and the same time, the Prophet stood up in anger on his carpet and declared that the man was making a plaything of the words of God, and made him take back his wife.

Even if we look to the deeds of the Prophet's companions, it is quite clear from the Hadith that the same was followed during Caliph Abu Bakr's times and the first two years of Caliph Umar and it was only to meet any exigency that Caliph Umar had started treating pronouncement of three divorces in one sitting as final and irrevocable:

i. Caliph Umar, finding that the checks imposed by the Prophet on the facility of repudiation interfered with the indulgence of their caprice, endeavoured to find an escape from the strictness of the law, and found in the pliability of the jurists a loophole to effect their purpose.
ii. When the Arabs conquered Syria, Egypt, Persia etc. and expressed their desire to marry them, these women insisted that they should first divorce their existing wife instantaneously.
iii. The Arabs readily accepted the condition since they knew that under Islam such divorce would not take effect and thus they would be able to marry women without having to divorce their existing wives. These incidents were reported to the second caliph, Hazrat Umar.
iv. In order prevent such misuse, Caliph Umar decreed that mere repetition of the word talaq thrice in one sitting would constitute a final and irrevocable divorce. Therefore, it was a mere administrative measure implemented by Caliph Umar to ensure that the provisions of the Holy Quran and Sunnah are not misused.

Triple Talaq as per Tafsir (Commentary on the Holy Quran)

In absence of any specific provision in the Holy Quran relating to instantaneous talaq, looking into the various *tafsir* (commentaries on the Holy Quran) becomes all the more important to understand if such form of instantaneous talaq is merely non-Islamic, or rather un-Islamic. Thus, the following section has extracts from various *tafsir*s which expand the various specific provisions of the Quran relating to divorce in general and triple talaq in particular to gather the true essence of the Quranic verses quoted above in the section on "Procedure of Talaq as per the Sources of Muslim Law":

Qur'an Tafsir Ibn Kathir (Vol. 1)[24] states as follows:

Divorce is Thrice.

This honorable Ayah abrogated the previous practice in the beginning of Islam, when the man had the right to take back his divorced wife even if he had divorced her a hundred times, as long as she was still in her Iddah (waiting period). This situation was harmful for the wife, and this is why Allah made the divorce thrice, where the husband is allowed to take back his wife after the first and the second divorce (as long as she is still in her Iddah). The divorce becomes irrevocable after the third divorce, as Allah said:

The divorce is twice, after that, either you retain her on reasonable terms or release her with kindness.

Pronouncing Three Divorces at the same Time is Unlawful.

The last Ayah we mentioned was used as evidence to prove that it is not allowed to pronounce three divorces at one time. What further proves this ruling is that Mahmud bin Labid has stated–as An-Nasa'i recorded–that Allah's Messenger was told about a man who pronounced three divorces on his wife at one time, so the Prophet stood up while angry and said:

The Book of Allah is being made the subject of jest while I am still amongst you.

A man then stood up and said, "Should I kill that man, O Messenger of Allah"[25]

Various scholars have thrown light on the condition precedent to divorce as ordained in the Holy Quran making it quite relevant in the present context. Sura IV verse 35 of the Holy Quran ordains: "If ye fear a breach Between them twain, Appoint two arbiters. One from his family, And the other from hers; If they wish for peace; God will cause Their reconciliation: For God hath full knowledge, And is acquainted With all things."

The commentary of Abdullah Yusuf Ali on the above-quoted verse states:

An excellent plan for settling family disputes, without too much publicity or mud-throwing, or resort to the chicaneries of the law. The Latin countries recognize this plan in their legal system. It is a pity that Muslims do not resort to it universally, as they should. The arbiters from each family would know the idiosyncrasies of both parties, and would be able, with God's help, effect a real reconciliation.[26]

Maulana Muhammad Ali, another noted commentator states the following on the above-quoted verse from the Holy Quran requiring appointment of arbiters for settlement of marital discord:

This verse lays down the procedure to be adopted when a case for divorce arises. It is not for the husband to put away his wife; it is the business of the judge to decide the case. Nor should the divorce case be made too public. The Judge is required to appoint two arbitrators, one belonging to the wife's family and the other to the husband's. These two arbitrators will find out the facts but their objective must be to effect a reconciliation between the parties. If all hopes of reconciliation fail, a divorce is allowed. But the final decision rests with the judge who is legally entitled, to pronounce a divorce. Cases were decided in accordance with the directions contained in this verse in the early days of Islam.[27]

In his book *The Religion of Islam*, Maulana Muhammad Ali further observes:

From what has been said above, it is clear that not only must there be a good cause for divorce, but that all means to effect reconciliation must have been exhausted before resort is had to this extreme measure. The impression that a Muslim husband may put away his wife at his mere caprice, is a grave distortion of the Islamic institution of divorce.[28]

Elsewhere divorce is thus discouraged: 'If you hate them [i.e., your wives] it may be that you dislike a thing while Allah has placed abundant good in it.' Remedies are also suggested to avoid divorce so long as possible. 'And if you fear a breach between the two (i.e., the husband and the wife), then appoint a judge from his people and a judge from her people. If they both desire agreement, Allah will effect harmony between them,' (4:35). It was due to such teachings of the Quran that the Prophet declared divorce to be the most hateful of all permitted things... The mentality of the Muslim is to face the difficulties of the married life along with its comforts, and to avoid disturbing the disruption of the family relations as long as possible, turning to divorce only as a last resort.[29]

He further states:

The principle of divorce spoken of in the Quran, and which in fact includes to a greater or less extent all causes, is the decision no longer to live together as husband and wife. In fact, marriage itself is nothing but an agreement to live together as husband and wife, and when either of the parties finds itself unable to agree to such a life, divorce must follow. It is not, of course, meant that every disagreement between them would lead to divorce; it is only the disagreement to live any more as husband and wife[30]...

Fyzee has also denounced talaq as "absurd and unjust".[31]

Therefore, we find that innovations like *talaq-ul-bidat* do not have any place either in the Quran or in the Sunnah.

Now the question arises that if such innovations as *bidat* and *zindiq* are not provided under Quran or Sunnah, how do these concepts develop and what is their status? From an anthropological perspective, this gap between law and local practice can be attributed to the historical development of Islamic society, wherein Islam slowly came to exist side by side in societies with other systems of belief. That is the reason why we find that some people lived their lives closer to the Islamic ideal than others. Moreover, as time goes by, people following the custom or usage start attaching different meanings to it. Therefore, such a custom or usage may not have anything to do with the Scripture and the law and may still have been in vogue because of sheer accretion; yet, it may have been accepted to this extent by society, that it came to be wrongly perceived as a part of the religious/legal system. So, saint worship may have developed due to any reason or even superstition, and may well be seen as a part of religion by some Muslims who practise it. However, such practices are eventually seen as giving way to the Islamic ideal as laid down by the basic tenants. Thus, many anthropologists are of the view that all such forms of customs and practices, like worshipping of saints, traces of caste, etc. are mere temporary anomalies, which would eventually be eliminated. For those scholars who see law to stand above the society as a standard of perfection, the desire to follow the true path is so strong that with the spread of the knowledge of Islamic law, the non-Islamic or false practices get ousted.

Be that as it may, in order to understand if the concept of triple talaq is one such practice, it is important to get the entire picture and see how the jurists under different schools have interpreted triple talaq.

Treatment of Triple Talaq by Jurists Under Different Schools

There are four main maslaq (schools of Sunni jurisprudence) among the Sunnis: Hanafi (majority of Indian Muslims), Maliki, Shafi'i, and Hanbali. There are conspicuous differences in interpretation among these schools and no clear conflict of law principles.

The four Sunni maslaq are the Hanafi established by Imam Abu Hanifa (702–72) followed in the Fertile Crescent,[32] Iraq, Turkey, lower Egypt, Afghanistan, and India. Maliki was established by Imam Malik Ibn Anas (711–95) and is followed in North Africa, while Shafi'i, established by Imam Al-Shafi'i (767–820), has followers in lower Egypt, Syria, India, and Indonesia. Finally, Hanbali, established by followers of Imam Ahmed ibn Hanbal of Baghdad (780–855), is followed in Saudi Arabia. The Ahl-e-Hadith seems to be an offshoot of the early Hanafi school and proponents of this school of thought can be described as strict constructionists. The Salafis that we hear of in the context of Syria are from this school.

In addition, there are three Shia schools as well. As is apparent from the timeline of the major schools, they were formed more than eighty years after the passing of the Prophet and therefore were able to undertake analogical reasoning with the help of Hadith recorded by way of hearsay.

The Ahl-e-Hadith (people of the Hadith) is a religious movement that regards the Holy Quran, the Sunnah, and the Hadith, to be the only true sources of Islam. They hold that no other source can serve as a source of religious authority and oppose any developments introduced into Islam after the earliest days of the faith, particularly the introduction of *taqlid* (the following of legal precedent). Instead, they favour ijtihad based on the original sources. Though this movement began in northern India in the mid-nineteenth century, adherents hold the same views as the early Ahl al-Hadith (late second and third centuries of Islam; late eighth and ninth centuries CE) movement. In more recent times, the movement has expanded to Pakistan, Bangladesh, and Afghanistan, garnering support from Saudi Arabia. The movement has been compared to Saudi Wahhabism or a variation on the Wahhabi movement, but the followers claim that the former is distinct from the latter.

The general impression is that the Hanafi school of law holds triple talaq to be valid and that three pronouncements shall amount to three separate divorces and shall result in a *mughallazah* or final divorce.

A reading of two of the works—*Al-Fiqh al-Absat* and *Al-Fiqh al-Akbar*—attributed to Abu Hanifa (the founder of the Hanafi school of jurisprudence) makes no mention of triple talaq or *talaq-e-bidat*. However, the following portions imply that there was, in fact, no clear guidance that they held it to be valid in all circumstances:

Abu Mutee said, 'I said, "So inform me about the most virtuous Fiqh." Abu Haneefah said, "That a man learns Imaan in Allaah

Ta`aalaa, the legislations, the Sunan, the Hudood (prescribed punishments), the disagreements of the Ummah and its consensus."'[33]

This shows that Abu Hanifa himself felt that it was important not just to look at what was said in consensus (that is, by the majority), but also by those in disagreement (that is, minority opinions).

He (Imaam Abu Haneefah) said, 'Hammaad narrated to us from Ibraaheem, from ibn Mas`ood that he used to say, "Indeed, the worst of matters are the newly invented ones. Every newly invented matter is a Bid`ah (Innovation), every Bid`ah is deviation and every deviation is in the fire."'[34]

Here we should remember that triple talaq or *talaq-e-bidat* is, by name and nature, an innovation—it is a practice of pre-Islamic Arabs that was made to survive despite the Prophet's dislike of it. Thus, Abu Hanifa would have seen such a practice as a sin and a deviation from the *fiqh*.

Abu Hanifa explained the principles which he followed in his ijtihad and to which he bound himself in derivation of rules. He said:

I follow Allah's Book when I find a rule in it. When I do not find a rule in it, I follow the Sunnah of Allah's Messenger (PBUH) and sound traditions from him which has been transmitted by the reliable persons. When I do not find a rule in Allah's Book nor in the Sunnah of Allah's Messenger, I follow the opinion of [the way] of the Companions I wish, and leave the opinion of anyone [I] wish. Then I do not go beyond their opinions to follow the opinion of others. When the matter comes to Ibrahim, al-Sha'bi, al-Hassan ibn Sirin, Sa'id ibn al-Musayyab, and he mentioned the names of some men who exercised ijtihad, I have the right to exercise ijtihad, as they did.[35]

If Abu Hanifa himself felt it was his task to introspect upon the words of the Prophet and his Companions, then why must scholars today take his word as gospel, instead of conducting the same exercise themselves? Even then he did not necessarily follow the words of all the Companions, but rather took those that he believed accorded with his understandings of the Holy Quran.

According to Ibn Taymiah,[36] any pronouncement of divorce made by pronouncing it thrice in one go by saying, "I divorce you three times or thrice" or any other similar expression, shall constitute only one pronouncement of divorce. Ibn Ishaq, Tawus, Akramah, and Ibn Abbas also hold the same view.[37]

Even those Hanafi jurists who see three instantaneous pronouncements to constitute a final, irrevocable divorce state that the reason for doing so is that in contemporary times, when people make three pronouncements together, they mean three divorces and do so with the intention to make it an irrevocable divorce. However, it may be pointed out that this interpretation of Hanafi jurists is not in line with what is ordained in the Holy Quran and the Sunnah, which provides for arbitration and a reconciliation period in the form of iddat to be observed before the divorce can be treated as final and irrevocable.

Hajjaj bin Artat (a narrator of one of the Hadiths of Ayesha and a Hanafi jurist) and Muhamad ibn Muqatil (a third-generation Hanafi jurist) both considered triple talaq invalid. The first stated that it did not even count as one divorce, while the latter was of the view that it would be considered as one revocable divorce or *talaq-i-raj'i*.

Howerver, if one goes by general consensus, the Hanafi and the Shafi'i Schools hold that talaq in bidat form is effective, even "though in its commission the man incurs a sin". Shias and the Malikis do not recognize the validity of the *talaq-ul-bidat*, while the Hanafi and the Shafi'i agree in holding that a divorce is effective, if pronounced in the *bidat* form, "though in its commission the man incurs a sin".[38] According to Shia law, there is general consensus that triple divorce at one time will be counted as only one divorce though it is pronounced in several numbers and the Imamia sect of Shia has faith that such divorce is no divorce.

All these schools allow revocation; that is, a husband who has suddenly and under inexplicable circumstances pronounced the formula against his wife, can revoke it any time before the three tuhrs have expired. When the power of recantation is lost, the separation or talaq becomes *bain* (irrevocable); while it continues, the talaq is simply *rajaat* or revocable.

3

Indian Courts and Muslim Personal Law

The Indian judiciary has dealt with the concept of triple talaq as early as 1905, in the matter of *Sara Bai v. Rabia Bai*[1] wherein the Bombay High Court recognized this form of talaq as irrevocable.

In *Saiyid Rashid Ahmad v. Mussammat Anisa Khatun*[2] the Privy Council held that three talaqs pronounced at one time would be valid and effective. The Court stated that the parties therein were Sunni Muhammedans and were thus "governed by the ordinary Hanafi law". In the opinion of their Lordships:

> the law of divorce applicable in such a case is correctly stated by Sir RK Wilson, in his Digest of Anglo-Muhammadan Law (6th edition) at p. 139 as follows:

The divorce called talak may be either irrevocable (bain) or revocable (rajjat). A talak bain, while it always operates as an immediate and complete dissolution of the marriage bond, differs as to one of its ulterior effects according to the form in which it is pronounced, A talak bain may be effected by words addressed to the wife clearly indicating an intention to dissolve the marriage, either.

(a) Once, followed by abstinence from sexual intercourse, for the period called the iddat; or
(b) Three times during successive intervals of purity, i.e., between successive menstruations, no intercourse taking place during any of the three intervals; or
(c) Three times at shorter intervals, or even in immediate succession; or
(d) Once, by words showing a clear intention that the divorce shall immediately become irrevocable.

The first-named of the above methods is called ahsan (best), the second hasan (good), the third and fourth are said to be bidaat (sinful), but are nevertheless regarded by Sunni lawyers as legally valid.

Such rulings were often driven by the understanding of the judiciary in British India that Muslims believed their laws to have divine source and thus were wary of interfering with them to any great extent. However, in time judicial pronouncements began to more carefully consider the application of Islamic law and the writings of those that questioned the unbridled and arbitrary nature of an irrevocable divorce pronounced thrice in one sitting.

V.R. Krishna Iyer, J. stated in *A. Yousuf Rawther v. Sowramma*[3] that:

It is a popular fallacy that a Muslim male enjoys, under the Quranic law, unbridled authority to liquidate the marriage.

The whole Quran expressly forbids a man to seek pretexts for divorcing his wife, so long as she remains faithful and obedient to him, if they (namely, women) obey you, then do not seek a way against them. (Quran IV:34) The Islamic law gives to the man primarily the faculty of dissolving the marriage, if the wife, by her indocility or her bad character, renders the married life unhappy; but in the absence of serious reasons, no man can justify a divorce, either in the eye of religion or the law.

In *Rukia Khatun v. Abdul Khalique Laskar,*[4] Islam, J., the Chief Justice of the Guwahati High Court sitting on a Division Bench, referred to Sura IV Verse 35 of the Quran and held that:

[T]here is a condition precedent which must be complied with before the talaq is effected. The condition precedent if when the relationship between the husband and the wife is strained and the husband intends to give 'talaq' to his wife he must choose an arbiter from his side and the wife an arbiter from her side, and the arbiters must attempt at reconciliation, with a time gap so that the passions of the parties may calm down and reconciliation may be possible. If ultimately conciliation is not possible, the husband will be entitled to give 'talaq'. The 'talaq' must be for good cause and must not be at the mere desire, sweet will, whim and caprice of the husband. It must not be secret.

In the same case the Court cited the observations of Maulana Mohammad Ali that "it is clear that not only must there be a good cause for divorce, but that all means to effect reconciliation must have been exhausted before resort is had to this extreme measure. The impression that a Muslim husband may put away his wife at his mere caprice, is a grave distortion of the Islamic institution of divorce". Thus, in the Guwahati High court's opinion, the correct law of talaq as ordained by Holy Quran is:

i. that *'talaq'* must be for a reasonable cause; and
ii. that it must be preceded by an attempt at reconciliation between the husband and wife by two arbiters, one chosen by the wife from her family and the other by the husband from his.
iii. if their attempts fail, *'talaq'* may be effected.

Subsequent to the above judgments, there were two streams of decisions by this Honourable Court, as also the various High Courts, that clarified the legal position in respect of instantaneous talaq. One set of decisions culminated in the decision of *Shamim Ara v. State of U.P. & Another,*[5] wherein this Honourable Court approved the decisions in *A. Yusuf Rawther v. Sowramma,*[6] *Jiauddin Ahmed v. Anwara Begum*[7], *and Rukia Khatun v. Abdul Khalique Laskar.*

The *Shamim Ara* decision is applicable to the three main types of talaq, that is, *talaq-i-ahsan, talaq-i-hasan,* and *talaq-i-bidat*. The *Shamim Ara* judgment settled the law that no form of Muslim talaq can be considered valid if it is not proved with clarity that it was for a reasonable cause and all the preceding attempts at resolving and reconciling differences were carried out before the pronouncement was made. Further, the pronouncement itself as well as its communication to the wife required convincing proof. Subsequent assertions in pleadings of a divorce pronounced in the past as it were, was unacceptable. This ruling was by itself a guard against a spur-of-the-moment divorce. It laid to rest the position taken by some schools that even an instantaneous talaq proclaimed in a state of intoxication, anger, or in jest was valid.

The other set of decisions have taken the issue of instantaneous talaq frontally, directly, and exclusively. This set of decisions have held that talaq by the husband in one sitting, whether through a single irrevocable pronouncement or through three simultaneous pronouncements, does not have the effect of granting divorce to the wife. It is clear now that each of these decisions stands overturned; so I shall not dwell upon them here.

The concept of triple talaq was challenged again in 2008 when Badar Durrez Ahmed, J. came to the conclusion that "triple talaq (talaq-e-bidaat), even for sunni muslims be regarded as one revocable talaq".[8] In *Masroor Ahmed* Justice Ahmed, as His Lordship then was, made a close examination of the sanctity of triple talaq in paragraphs 23–38 of the judgment and came to the aforesaid conclusion based on the reasoning that this form of talaq did not fulfil the requirements for an effective divorce under the teachings of the Quran. The question that was raised about this judgment by the Board was that it is not open to the Court to sift through millions of words that have been written on the subject and distil the truth from them. But surely there was nothing else that the Court can do in the circumstances and going by the findings it did a good job, keeping in line with what all the Islamic countries and others have done.

Justice Badar Durrez Ahmed had, after examining the whole conspectus of Muslim Personal Law and judicial decisions in this respect, held as follows:

Sanctity and effect of Talaq-e-bidaat or triple talaq.

24. There is no difficulty with ahsan talaq or hasan talaq. Both have legal recognition under all fiqh schools, sunni or shia. The difficulty lies with triple talaq which is classed as bidaat (an innovation). Generally speaking, the shia schools do not recognise triple talaq as bringing about a valid divorce. There

is, however, difference of opinion even within the sunni schools as to whether the triple talaq should be treated as three talaqs, irrevocably bringing to an end the marital relationship or as one rajai (revocable) talaq, operating in much the same way as an ahsan talaq.

25. When a difference of opinion is discernible within a particular school, normally the dominant opinion is taken as representative of the school. But, this does not mean that a qazi, when required to render a decision in a specific case, cannot, in the interest of justice and equity, adopt the view of the minority within the school. It is also interesting to note that traditionally the qazi gave the ruling based upon the school which he followed. So, if he was a follower of the hanafi school he decided cases on the basis of hanafi fiqh. Consequently, if a dispute were to be brought to a qazi who followed shafei fiqh he would decide according to shafei precepts. In India, the secular courts while applying muslim law to muslims in accordance with Section 2 of the 1937 Act have adopted the principle of applying the fiqh to which the parties belong. Meaning thereby, that hanafi principles would be applied to adherents of the hanafi school and ithna ashari law to ithna asharis and so on. This, however, has not been strictly followed, perhaps in ignorance. Clearly, a qazi or a judge is permitted to apply a minority view within a school of fiqh to adherants of that school. He is also permitted to apply a view taken by a school of law of which the parties are not members of. This can be done in the interest of justice and equity and to avoid hardship to any one or both the parties provided, of course, that what the judge proposes to do is not contrary to a basic tenet of Islam or the Quran or a ruling or saying or act of prophet Muhammad.

26. It is accepted by all schools of law that talaq-e-bidaat is sinful. Yet some schools regard it as valid. Courts in India have also held it to be valid. The expression – bad in theology but valid in law – is often used in this context. The fact remains that it is considered to be sinful. It was deprecated by prophet Muhammad.

It is definitely not recommended or even approved by any school. It is not even considered to be a valid divorce by shia schools. There are views even amongst the sunni schools that the triple talaq pronounced in one go would not be regarded as three talaqs but only as one. Judicial notice can be taken of the fact that the harsh abruptness of triple talaq has brought about extreme misery to the divorced women and even to the men who are left with no chance to undo the wrong or any scope to bring about a reconciliation. It is an innovation which may have served a purpose at a particular point of time in history but, if it is rooted out such a move would not be contrary to any basic tenet of Islam or the Quran or any ruling of the Prophet Muhammad.

27. In this background, I would hold that a triple talaq (talaq-e-bidaat), even for sunni muslims be regarded as one revocable talaq. This would enable the husband to have time to think and to have ample opportunity to revoke the same during the iddat period. All this while, family members of the spouses could make sincere efforts at bringing about a reconciliation. Moreover, even if the iddat period expires and the talaq can no longer be revoked as a consequence of it, the estranged couple still has an opportunity to re-enter matrimony by contracting a fresh nikah on fresh terms of mahr etc.

In *Mohd. Naseem Bhat v. Bilquees Akhter and Ors*[9] the Court dismissed review in the matter of the same name and reiterated that:

The power to pronounce talaq [...] is not unbridled but subject to the limitations provided under Shariat Law itself. Two of the limitations that talaq, if necessary, is to be pronounced not in a whimsical or arbitrary manner but for a genuine reason and that a serious and sincere effort for reconciliation between the estranged spouses, must precede pronouncement of talaq, are substantive in character, to be proved to successfully resist an action brought by wife to enforce a right based on her claimed marital status, while other two conditions viz. talaq, even where there is a genuine reason and the reconciliation efforts fail, is to be pronounced in presence of two witnesses endued with justice and during the prescribed period (purity) touch the procedure and the last may be proved by mere statement of the person, insisting on divorce and resisting the claim.

As recently as December 2016, the High Court of Kerala, in *Nazeer v. Shemeema* case[10], stated that:

8. It is to be noted that Qur'an nowhere approves triple talaq in one utterance and on the other hand promotes conciliation as best method to resolve the marital discord. The method and procedure of divorce as [mentioned] above has been referred to by all leading Islamic scholars. They also have frowned upon triple talaq in single utterance to effect divorce saying that it revolts against Allah's law. One of the eminent Islamic scholars Sheikh Yusuf al Qaradawi in his book 'The Lawful and the Prohibited in Islam' refers to method of divorce and holds that triple talaq in single utterance is against God's law.

4

Reforms in Islamic States

In most Muslim countries across the world, domestic law no longer recognizes triple talaq as a valid form of divorce. The route they follow is to treat three pronouncements as one single declaration. A survey of the following provisions in various legislations of such states shows that the Islamic world has increasingly come to realize that triple talaq does not have any foundation in the teachings of Islam; and certainly not any place in the modern world under Islamic law.

In most of these countries, three pronouncements are taken as one single pronouncement of talaq, much like the ratio of *Masroor Ahmed*.

The following survey of the major Muslim countries of the world shows that the laws in these nations support the proposition that triple talaq does not find a place in Islam:

1. **EGYPT** (The seat of Al Azhar University, which is considered one of the top centres of Islamic learning): Articles 356 and 557 of Law No. 25 (1929), as amended by Law No. 100 of 1985 Concerning Certain Provisions on Personal Status in Egypt, expressly provides that triple talaq will be considered as one.
2. **IRAQ** (A majority of the population is Shia, but was long ruled by a Sunni head of State): Article 37(2) of Law No. 188 of 1959, The Law of Personal Status of Iraq states that "[t]hree verbal or gestural repudiations pronounced at once will count as only one divorce".
3. **SUDAN:** Section 360 of Sudanese Manshur-i-Qadi al-Qudat provides that triple talaq shall be considered as one. Article 3, Shariah Circular No. 41/1935 of Sudan states that pronouncement of all divorces by the husband is revocable except the third one, along with a divorce before consummation of marriage, and a divorce for consideration.
4. **PAKISTAN** (Majority being Sunnis of the Hanafi school): Section 7 of Muslim Family Law Ordinance 1961 provides that the traditional form of divorce is not in force in its original form. According to said provision:

   (1) Any man who wishes to divorce his wife shall, as soon as may be after the pronouncement of talaq in any form whatsoever, give the Chairman notice in writing of his having done so, and shall supply a copy thereof to the wife.

   [...]

(2) Save as provided in sub-section (5), a talaq unless revoked earlier, expressly or otherwise, shall not be effective until the expiration of ninety days from the day on which notice under sub-section (1) is delivered to the Chairman.

(3) Within thirty days of the receipt of notice under sub-section (1), the Chairman shall constitute an Arbitration Council for the purpose of bringing about a reconciliation between the parties, and the Arbitration Council shall take all steps necessary to bring about such reconciliation.

5. **SYRIA:** Under Article 92 of Law No. 34 of the Law of Personal Status of Syria of 1953, if a divorce is coupled with a number, 33 expressly or implied, not more than one divorce shall take place and every divorce shall be revocable except a third divorce, a divorce before consummation, and a divorce with consideration. Further, such a divorce would be considered irrevocable.

6. **MOROCCO, AFGHANISTAN, LIBYA, KUWAIT, YEMEN:** These countries adopted similar laws in 1958, 1977, 1984, 1984, and 1992 respectively:
Article 51 Book Two of the Mudawwana of 1957 and 1958 of Morocco.
Sections 145 and 146 of the Civil Law of 4 January 1977 of Afghanistan.
Section 33(d) of Law No. 10 of 1984, Concerning the Specific Provisions on Marriage and Divorce and their Consequences in Libya.
Section 109 of Law No. 51 of 1984 regarding al-Ahwal al-Shakhsiyah (Personal Law) in Kuwait.
Article 64 of the Republican Decree Law No. 20 of 1992, Concerning Personal Status of Yemen.

7. **UAE, QATAR, BAHRAIN:** Despite the impression of these countries being overtly orthodox, they have adopted similar measures under their Personal Law statutes.
   Section 103(1) of Qanun al-Ahwal al-Shakhsiya (Personal Law) of UAE No. 28 of 2005.
   Section 108 of Qanun al-Usrah (Family Law) of Qatar, No. 22 of 2006.
   Section 88(C) of Law No. 19 of 2009 regarding Qanun Ahkam al-Usrah of Bahrain.
8. **SRI LANKA** (A Buddhist majority country with substantial Muslim and Hindu minorities in the north and the east. In that sense their experience seems closest to our own): The Marriage and Divorce (Muslim) Act, 1951, as amended up to 2006, provides that a husband intending to divorce his wife "shall give notice of his intention to the Qauzi [Qazi]" who shall attempt reconciliation between the spouses "with the help the relatives of the parties and of the elders and other influential Muslims of the area".

However, if after 30 days of giving notice to the Quazi, attempts at reconciling the spouses remain fruitless, "the husband, if he desires to proceed with the divorce, shall pronounce the talak in the presence of the Quazi and two witnesses".

There is also a concept of umma in Islam that technically goes beyond nation states. However, with the growth of the modern states it has become a theoretical construct rather than a reality. But a certain level of empathy remains on the Palestine issue and the concept of umma was wrongly and unsuccessfully sought by Pakistan over the decades on Kashmir (Indian Jammu & Kashmir). More recently, the tension between Iran and Saudi Arabia on one hand and the complicated politics of Iraq, Syria, Lebanon, and Yemen, not to mention the Islamic State (ISIS) has left little semblance of the umma in the real world.

In the following list, India, Nigeria, Ethiopia, China, Russia, and the Philippines have large Muslim populations, but they are not a majority in these countries. For other listed countries, the Muslim population has an overwhelming majority.[1]

Indonesia	2,25,000,000 (87.2%)
Pakistan	20,41,94,370 (96.4%)
India	18,90,00,000 (14.2%)
Bangladesh	14,86,07,00 (90.4%)
Nigeria	9,38,39,000 (41–50%)
Iran	8,07,50,000 (99.7%)
Turkey	7,46,60,000 (98.6%)
Egypt	7,38,00,000 (90%)
Algeria	4,04,00,000 (98.2–99%)
Morocco	3,23,81,000 (99%)
Iraq	3,11,08,000 (99%)
Sudan	3,90,27,950 (97%)
Saudi Arabia	3,18,78,000 (97.1%)
Afghanistan	2,90,47,100 (99.8%)
Ethiopia	2,50,37,646 (34%)
Uzbekistan	2,68,33,000 (96.5%)
Yemen	2,40,23,000 (99%)

China	2,20,00,000–5,00,00,000 (1.8%)
Syria	1,73,76,000 (82.9%)
Malaysia	1,95,00,000 (61.4%)
Russia	94,00,000–2,00,00,000 (6.5–15%)
Niger	1,95,02,214 (98.3%)
The Philippines	50,00,000–1,07,00,000 (5–11%)
Somalia	92,31,000 (98.9%)

Muslims also live in, but also have an official status in the following regions:

Africa: North African countries such as Morocco, Algeria, Tunisia, Libya, Egypt, and Sudan; Northeast African countries like Somalia, Eritrea, Ethiopia, and Djibouti; and West African countries like Mali, Senegal, The Gambia, Guinea, Guinea-Bissau, Burkina Faso, Sierra Leone, Niger, Nigeria, Chad, Mauritania, Ghana, Ivory Coast, Cameroon, Liberia, Comoros, Togo, and Benin.

Asia: In Central Asia, countries such as Kazakhstan, Kyrgyzstan, Tajikistan, Turkmenistan, Uzbekistan, and Xinjiang (China); in Southwest Asia, Arab nations such as Saudi Arabia, Iraq, Oman, United Arab Emirates, Kuwait, Bahrain, and Yemen, and non-Arab nations such as Turkey, Northern Cyprus, Iran, and Azerbaijan. In South Asia, it's Afghanistan, Pakistan, Bangladesh, and the Maldives, and Indonesia, Brunei, Malaysia, and Singapore in Southeast Asia. While in East Asia, it is parts of China (Ningxia).

Europe: Albania, Bosnia and Herzegovina, and Kosovo, Russia (North Caucasus and the Volga region), and Ukraine (especially in the Crimea).

The countries of southwest Asia and some in northern and northeastern Africa are considered part of the Greater Middle East. In Russia's Chechnya, Dagestan, Kabardino-Balkaria, Karachay-Cherkessia, Ingushetia, Tatarstan, and Bashkortostan, Muslims are in the majority.

On several occasions during arguments on the *Triple Talaq* case, the then Chief Justice enquired about the situation in Saudi Arabia, but somehow the point was not picked up by any counsel. Much later, while the judgment was awaited, I had the opportunity to speak to the Saudi ambassador to India, who promptly confirmed that triple talaq was not recognized in the Kingdom and even narrated the story of having consulted the Grand Mufti upon being referred facts.

The Board counsel dismissed these developments as being inconsequential to Indian law. However, that implies repudiation of the accepted concept of umma or the community of the faithful the world over. India has made great contributions to the world of Islam and remains the third-largest population of Muslims after Indonesia and Bangladesh, though for historical reasons, we did not become a member of the Organization of Islamic Countries (OIC). Although national aspirations can at times pull in different directions, in the matter of association with religion, there is little justification of separate and segmented perception.

Legislation on subjects of concern to Muslims of India has been somewhat sparingly introduced. The base was provided by the Shariat Application Act, 1937, essentially an attempt to clarify that in matters of family and inheritance, the Shariah law would be applicable, albeit without any additional customs and usages that might have attached themselves to original principles. The Board counsel ventured to suggest that this was to weed out customs that Hindu converts had brought with them on embracing Islam. That might not be wrong, but it does not reflect the entire truth. Islam has obviously evolved in the subcontinent, often influenced by local conditions, as happens anywhere. The indigenous Sufi movement in India, although closely connected with the spiritual movements of Iran and Afghanistan, has a close resonance with the Bhakti movement. Much of this might not find favour in the Saudi system. But as Francis Robinson observes, Shariah had to co-exist with customs perceived as laws in South Asia as indeed in other Muslim societies throughout the history of Islam. All such tolerance came to an end in India by the time the Shariat Application Act, 1937 came to be passed. Robinson traces similar development in Malaysia and Indonesia as well as in Saudi Arabia.

Section 2 of The Muslim Personal (Sharia) Law Act, 1937 reads as follows:

Section 2 Application of Personal law to Muslims:

Notwithstanding any custom or usage to the contrary, in all questions (save questions relating to agricultural land) regarding intestate succession, special property of females, including personal property inherited or obtained under contract or gift or any other provision of Personal Law, marriage, dissolution of marriage, including talaq, ila, zihar, lian, khula and mubaraat, maintenance, dower, guardianship, gifts, trusts and trust properties, and wakfs (other than charities and charitable institutions and charitable and religious endowments) the rule of decision in cases where the parties are Muslims shall be the Muslim Personal Law (Shariat).

The Dissolution of Muslim Marriages Act, 1939, the first attempt at legislation after the path-breaking clarification in 1937, in essence gave statutory framework to the rights of divorce or dissolution that Muslim women have under Shariah. The Objects and Reasons of the Act once again state that it is to consolidate and clarify as indeed to remove doubts about the effect of renunciation of Islam. What is however more important is that in passing this legislation, the legislature specifically recognized that to obviate the harshness of Shariah according to one maslaq, it was open to borrow from another maslaq.

It must be pointed out that in both cases, legislation was passed on the insistence of the Muslim clergy. Since then, however, there has been no similar popular demand for further legislation; if anything, there have been repeated assertions for a hands-off approach by the Parliament. It was therefore somewhat surprising that during the hearing of this case the Board's counsel should have expressed willingness to Parliament interceding. What made it more puzzling is that while the Court was told to steer clear of Personal Law of 1,400-year vintage, there was an admission that it was not out of bounds for legislature! Perhaps it was this concession that persuaded the then Chief Justice to carve out the path for appropriate legislation. But then it must be recalled that the Attorney General had sought a clean slate with all forms of talaq invalidated with a promise that Parliament would put down a comprehensive law to replace it.

As a constitutional court it was inevitable that the Bench would be invited to examine the entire issue from a constitutional perspective, or what the Attorney General described as "constitutional morality". Inevitably, that raises our understanding and reading of the Constitution. This is a vast subject and the Supreme Court has much dicta dealing with it. But I felt it was important to point out that constitutional morality is quite different from popular morality that can be gleaned from public-opinion surveys and referenda. In the context, I gave the Court copies of the inaugural lecture for the Chair of Jurisprudence at Oxford by the late Professor Ronald Dworkin. The distinguished philosopher, in dealing with the complex idea of "Hard Cases" (the title of the lecture), imagines two kinds of judges: the first is called Hercules, with the amazing intellectual prowess of a super judge; the other, Herbert, after the former occupier of the Chair—H.L.A. Hart—whose linguistic theory of judicial decision-making had been challenged by Dworkin.

Drawing from intuition and experience of how judges in the common law system approach difficult legal problems, Dworkin arrives at the following conclusions:[2]

> We might therefore do well to consider how a philosophical judge might develop, in appropriate cases, theories of what legislative purpose and legal principles require. We shall find that he would construct these theories in the same manner as a philosophical referee would construct the character of a game. I have invented, for this purpose, a lawyer of superhuman skill, learning, patience and acumen,whom I shall call Hercules.
>
> Hercules must suppose that it is understood in his community, though perhaps not explicitly recognized, that judicial decisions must be taken to be justified by arguments of principle rather than arguments of policy. He now sees that the familiar concept used by judges to explain their reasoning from precedent, the concept of certain principles that underline or are embedded in the common law, is itself only a metaphorical statement of

the rights thesis. He may henceforth use that concept in his decisions of hard common law cases. It provides a general test for deciding such cases that is like the chess referee's concept of the character of a game, and like his own concept of a legislative purpose. It provides a question – What set of principles best justifies the precedents? – that builds a bridge between the general justification of the practice of precedent, which is fairness, and his own decision about what that general justification requires in some particular hard case.

Dworkin then proceeds to examine the run-of-the-mill, conventional judge:

Let us imagine another judge, called Herbert, who accepts this theory of adjudication and proposes to follow it in his decisions. Herbert might believe both women have a background right to abort fetuses they carry, and that the majority of citizens think otherwise. The present objection argues that he must resolve that conflict in favor of democracy, so that, when he exercises his discretion to decide the abortion cases, he must decide in favor of the prohibitive statutes. Herbert might agree, in which case we should say that he has set aside his morality in favor of the people's morality. That is, in fact, a slightly misleading way to put the point. His own morality made the fact that the people held a particular view decisive; it did not withdraw in favor of the substance of that view.

Herbert did not consider whether to consult popular morality until he had fixed the legal rights of the parties. But, when Hercules fixes legal rights he has already taken the community's moral traditions into account, at least as these are captured in the whole institutional record that it is his office to interpret.

Of course, Hercules' techniques may sometimes require a decision that opposes popular morality on some issue. Suppose no justification of the earlier constitutional cases can be given that does not contain a liberal principle sufficiently strong to require a decision in favor of abortion. Hercules must then reach that decision, no matter how strongly popular morality condemns abortion. He does not, in this case, enforce his own convictions against the community's. He rather judges that the community's morality is inconsistent on this issue: its constitutional morality, which is the justification that must be given for its constitution as interpreted by its judges.

Let us attempt to examine this concept in our context. A Constitution Bench of this Honourable Court in *Manoj Narula v. Union of India*[3] expounded on the concept of constitutional morality (at Paras 74–76) as:

The Constitution of India is a living instrument with capabilities of enormous dynamism. It is a Constitution of India made for a progressive society. Working of such a Constitution of India depends upon the prevalent atmosphere and conditions. Dr Ambedkar had, throughout the Debate, felt that the Constitution of India can live and grow on the bedrock of Constitutional morality. Speaking on the same, he said: 'Constitutional morality is not a natural sentiment. It has to be cultivated. We must realize that our people are yet to learn it. Democracy in India is only a top-dressing on an Indian soil, which is essentially undemocratic.' The principle of Constitutional morality basically means to bow down to the norms of the Constitution of India and not to act in a manner which would become violative of the rule of law or reflectible of action in an arbitrary manner. It actually works at the fulcrum and guides as a laser beam in institution building. The traditions and conventions have to grow to sustain the value of such a morality. The democratic values survive and become successful where the people at large and the persons-in-charge of the institution are strictly guided by the Constitutional parameters without paving the path of deviancy and reflecting in action the primary concern to maintain institutional integrity and the requisite Constitutional restraints. Commitment to the Constitution of India is a facet of Constitutional morality.

The Attorney General also added that "constitutional morality" strives for gender equality, dignity of women, and abandonment of patriarchal, anachronistic, and retrograde practices; a sweeping argument about constitutional morality that did not readily distinguish it from popular morality. Unfortunately, the only opportunity I had to address this concept with Dworkin's Herbert and Hercules came during the rejoinder arguments. By then the Court was beginning to wind up and knowing when to pick my battles, I apprised the Court of the learned author, armed them with copies of his work, and held my peace. One day certainly the Court will have to look at the theoretical framework of constitutional versus popular more carefully. Till then, those of us who think about the Constitution must, in humility, recall that the same Constitution has meant different things to different judges. It is, after all, the same court that protected the right to property in *Golakh Nath*,[4] yet accepted that the right might be taken away and that indeed the Constitution could be dramatically amended (subject to the Basic Structure doctrine); it was again the same Court that pronounced *ADM Jabalpur*[5] and *Maneka Gandhi*.[6] Thus, to assume that some version of constitutional values are obvious and incontestable might lead to surprises. Judgments in *Naz*,[7] *National Anthem*,[8] and *Love Jehad*[9] do not uniformly fit into a pattern with many of the Court's pronouncements on Articles 14 and 21. Constitutional morality therefore is far more complex than it is generally assumed and is sometimes wrongly associated with popular morality. The death penalty is an obvious example to test this thesis. And it is interesting that two recent judgments of the Supreme Court have sought to draw inspiration from Dworkin.

Although the Court did not proceed to tackle how Dworkin's "hard case" is to be handled interestingly in two other judgments pronounced within days of the *Triple Talaq* judgment, including the nine judges' Bench on Privacy,[10] the Court has conspicuously noticed the rights thesis. However, while Justice A.K. Sikri in *Binoy Vishwam*[11] seemed to have recognized the analytical insights of Dworkin, the nine judges took it to be a part of the Natural Law tradition. Although the conclusions arrived at are remarkable in their liberal expanse the analytical tools that Dworkin offers are invaluable, indeed imperative if the Court is to avoid mistakes, as in the *ADM Jabalpur* case, specifically overruled by the Nine Judges Bench.

5

Submissions before the Court

So far, this book has set out in brief some of the submissions of various parties/counsel appearing before the Court in the *Triple Talaq* matter, as well as my comments thereon. This section will conclude with my concise submissions before the Court. Being an intervener, I came before the Court with no Prayer per se. However, to be a friend to the Court (though not an appointed amicus), one must offer some solution, and not just be present to muddy the waters chasing one's 15 minutes of fame. Thus, I made the following submissions.

It Is Not the Role of the Court to Interpret Muslim Personal Law

The Supreme Court has time and again held that personal laws cannot be tested on the touchstone of Part III of the

Constitution. However, as I stated above, the Honourable Court, at present, need not have examined the broader issue of whether personal laws are part of the definition of "law in force" under Article 13 of the Constitution as indeed Justice Nariman finally opted to do. I had submitted that it is not the role of the Court to interpret de novo Muslim Personal Law, in this case Muslim law, but rather hold which interpretation is correct. The then Chief Justice remarked during the arguments that I had advised aloofness, and that finds place in his judgment as well. Our constitutional courts are familiar with the thin dividing line between plain interpretation of legislation (with the help of devices like the mischief rule,[1] purposive interpretation,[2] and the intent of Parliament[3]) and judicial legislation by an activist judiciary.

Under Muslim Personal Law, the religious heads or imams are called upon to decipher the teachings of the Quran and the Hadith, in particular conflicts. The imams resolve these conflicts not by deciding what the correct course of action is, *suo moto*, but by reading the sources, that is, the Holy Quran and the Hadith, and deciphering the correct interpretation/meaning of the same. Herein, the Court's role is no different from the application of any general or secular law—to look at the interpretations offered by scholars and imams and decide the correct one to apply to a given case. Inherent, self-imposed restrictions against what is described as judicial legislation would apply more vigorously to the matter of Personal Law. Just as the Court may have access to experts when hearing civil or criminal cases, and particularly under the Waqf Act, 1995 as amended in 2013, they would have access to experts in Islamic law when dealing with questions of Muslim Personal Law. They need not address questions by novel reasoning of their own. Further, as the Court stated in *Aga Mahomed Jaffer Bindaneem v. Koolsom Bee Bee and Others*,[4] "it would be wrong for the Court on a point of this kind [that is, in relation to Personal Law] to attempt to put their own construction on the Koran in opposition to the express ruling of commentators of such great antiquity and high authority".

Shamim Ara Did Not Decide the Question of Validity of Triple Talaq

Some who argued before the Court suggest that indeed the entire question of triple talaq had already been decided by the seminal case of *Shamim Ara*.[5] This, I submitted, is an incorrect reading of the case. In *Shamim Ara*, the salient holding of the Court was related to the pronouncement of talaq. The Court held that "*talaq to be effective has to be pronounced*" and that "[t]he term 'pronounce' means to proclaim, to utter formally, to utter rhetorically, to declare to, utter, to articulate." However, citing the case of *Rukia Khatun v. Abdul Khalique Laskar*[6] this Hon'ble Court stated that "the correct law of *talaq*, as ordained by Holy Quran, is: (i) that 'talaq' must be for a reasonable cause; and (ii) that it must be preceded by an attempt of reconciliation between the husband and the wife by two arbiters, one chosen by the wife from her family and the other by the husband from his. If their attempts fail, '*talaq*' may be effected." While *Shamim Ara* was in agreement with the observations of the High Courts, it did not actually comment on the validity of triple talaq per se, as that was not the question before them.

So the matter was still open to be decided by the Court.

Changes in Personal Law in Foreign Countries May Be a Guide to the Court While Considering the Present Issue

Islamic law the world over is guided by the same primary sources, that is, the Holy Quran and the Sunnah; their interpretation and application by other countries can be a valid guide for interpreting Muslim Personal Law in this country. While Muslim Personal Law is in some ways a peculiar creature of the Indian subcontinent, the religious heads in India in applying the law carry on an identical exercise as that carried out by officials and religious heads in other countries, that is, they look at the primary sources of Islam to find the solution to any issue; failing a resolution in the primary sources, a solution is found by consensus. Where consensus differs amongst different scholars, different schools are formed, which interpret or apply the law differently. While the majority of the religious leaders in India may subscribe to one such school (that is, Hanafi), this does not invalidate the guidance/opinion of the other schools of thought, which may be as valid. Changes in the application/interpretation of Personal Law are driven by a change in the consensus/thinking of different schools of jurists, that is, a change in the ijma. These changes do not reflect a new interpretation of the Holy Quran, which is by its nature absolute and timeless, but rather a change in the opinion of the true meaning of the words of the Holy Quran through deliberation. In other words, through the independent reasoning or the thorough exertion of a jurist's mental faculty towards gleaning the true meaning of the words of the Holy Quran (ijtihad). In these circumstances it is clear that the changes in Personal

Law in foreign countries may also be a consideration/guide in the interpretation of Muslim Personal Law in India.

To buttress the point, I briefly drew the attention of the Court to the relationship between national law and international law. In many cases, changes in national legislation are driven by international commitments or changes in international law. The legislature being supreme, no change in international law alone can bind a national legislature to change the law. However, changes in international law—particularly the signing of international treaties—can on many occasions be a persuasive, if not determinative, guide towards changes in the national law. Finally, the courts in India, including the Supreme Court, often refer to the judgments of foreign courts when looking at a corresponding issue of national law. While this is not a mandatory exercise, courts have often chosen to include the wisdom of their counterparts in other jurisdictions when considering a question of law before them. Foreign judgments may help guide our judiciary on similar or identical questions of law. Similarly, the Court may also look to the treatment in Muslim countries of the questions before the Court herein and seek guidance—though they are not bound by it—in the choice in other countries between the interpretations offered by various schools of Islamic jurisprudence.

Currently, Qazis Are Not Empowered to Act as an Adjudicatory Authority in Issues Relating to Marriage or Divorce under Muslim Personal Law

Although qazis were judicial and religious officers in the pre-British administration of law, their office fell into disuse with the advent of common law. They are not even empowered under the law in India to issue certificates of marriage or divorce. Their presence during either of the events does not validate the events and their absence does not invalidate them (*All Assam Muslim Marriage & Ors. v. State of Assam and Ors*[7]). Yet all marriages are solemnized by qazis who issue certificates and maintain the records in a register. On the other hand, the Board has set up several dozen Dar-ul-Qaza establishments headed by qazis, but these are not the ones who solemnize marriages. Essentially, these establishments deal with Muslim couples who want to separate and provide all assistance, including making efforts at reconciliation. Reportedly, 70 per cent of petitioners are women seeking khula and 30 per cent are men hoping to save their marriages. Clearly, therefore, the need is to ensure adjudication by qazis or Family Courts applying Shariah for the purpose.

Khula allows women to release themselves from the marital bond on offering to give up mehar to the husband or any other condition as consideration for release. The execution of a khula is subject to the husband's acceptance of the terms, but it is not clear if he can refuse entirely.

Directions were recently issued by the Madras High Court as well in *Mrs. Bader Sayeed Advocate v. Union of India*[8] regarding the certificates issued by qazis. Relying on Section 4 of the Kazis Act, 1880, the Court issued directions that for the purposes of legal proceedings, the certificate is only an opinion. The Board, which is respondent no. 9 in the *Mrs. Bader Sayeed Advocate*, has also taken this stand.

During oral arguments, some senior counsel and I raised the issue of some form of adjudicatory supervision. I had submitted that qazis, duly authorized so to act, may be given adjudicatory authority as envisioned in the entire scheme of marriage and divorce laid out in the Holy Quran and the Hadith and thus help safeguard the rights of both, the wife and husband as intended in the holy scriptures.

Triple Talaq Is No Part of Shariah

In response to a question posed by the Court during oral arguments—whether triple talaq should be considered a mere custom or usage (in the context of Section 2 of the Muslim Personal Law (Shariat) Application Act, 1937)—I submitted that this question was in fact a moot point.

As I have endeavoured to show through many preceding sections (see the sections on 'The Holy Quran' and 'The Sunnah' in Chapter 2), triple talaq finds no mention in the primary sources of Islam. In fact, in light of the entire scheme of marriage and divorce as laid down in the same, the concept of an instantaneous talaq is antithetical to the very teachings of Islam and the Prophet. Thus, triple talaq cannot be considered a part of the Shariah. In fact, as seen from the account of its enforcement under the second Caliph Hazrat Umar in Chapter 2, if anything it was made valid only to meet the exigencies of a particular situation and from there precipitated only through usage, never through any proclamation that it was an essential and integral part of the Islamic faith.[2]

Triple talaq can only be considered a creature of custom. One that most, if not all, sections of the worldwide Muslim community and most Muslim countries have recognized as *haram* or sin and thus not a valid form.

Furthermore, in the objects and reasons of the Act it states that the "introduction of Muslim Personal Law will automatically raise them [Muslim women] to the position to which they are naturally entitled". I submitted that the Prophet had an identical object when he brought the word of Allah to the pre-Islamic community, that is, to better the position of women, who were so badly mistreated by the pre-Islamic Arabs. Thus, the Court would only be fulfilling the purpose of the Act by recognizing that Muslim Personal Law or Shariah is, in fact, constituted of the wise and endearing words of the Holy Quran, and the teachings of the Prophet, that is, the Hadith.

Finally, in applying the interpretations or teachings of a particular school, the Court must recognize that no school is an infallible or immutable authority. Islamic jurists seek to interpret the primary sources of Islam either through ijma (consensus) or *ijtihaad* (introspection). In this they are informed by their own social, political, and cultural realities. Thus, different jurists may come to different conclusions at different times. The task of the Court should be to look at the various interpretation offered by Islamic jurists/authorities and seek to apply the one in the situation which best offers an equitable and just solution. Here this exercise has been well described by Badar Ahmad, J. in *Masroor Ahmad* as follows:

25. When a difference of opinion is discernible within a particular school, normally the dominant opinion is taken as representative of the school. But, this does not mean that a qazi [or indeed a court], when required to render a decision in a specific case, cannot, in the interest of justice and equity, adopt the view of the minority within the school. It is also interesting to note that traditionally the qazi gave the ruling based upon the school which he followed. So, if he was a follower of the hanafi school he decided cases on the basis of hanafi fiqh. Consequently, if a

dispute were to be brought to a qazi who followed shafei fiqh he would decide according to shafei precepts. In India, the secular courts while applying muslim law to muslims in accordance with section 2 of the 1937 Act have adopted the principle of applying the fiqh to which the parties belong. Meaning thereby, that hanafi principles would be applied to adherents of the hanafi school and ithna ashari law to ithna asharis and so on. This, however, has not been strictly followed, perhaps in ignorance. Clearly, a qazi or a judge is permitted to apply a minority view within a school of fiqh to adherants of that school. He is also permitted to apply a view taken by a school of law of which the parties are not members of. This can be done in the interest of justice and equity and to avoid hardship to any one or both the parties provided, of course, that what the judge proposes to do is not contrary to a basic tenet of Islam or the Quran or a ruling or saying or act of prophet Muhammad.

The door to such a pluralistic interpretation of Muslim Personal Law is in fact opened by the statement of the Hanafi jurists themselves, as recorded in the Objects and Reasons of the Act, which states that the teachings of another school may be applied where the teachings of the Hanafi school may cause hardship (as quoted in Chapter 2).

The Muslim Personal Law Board had argued that the Court must accept their view of faith and refrain from interfering with it on any ground, including constitutional scrutiny. It is a matter in which only the community can take a view or Parliament can take initiative to deal with it. It seems strange that a matter of faith is not immutable but variable at the hands of community or Parliament and yet the Court must steer clear of it. If triple talaq is intrinsic to faith and therefore beyond the interference of Courts, it seems inexplicable that the Board speaks of working to educate people to refrain from resorting to it. The Board also argued that triple talaq can be mutually agreed to be shunned in the nikahnama, although to exclude other forms of talaq would be un-Islamic and therefore not permissible. How can one "essential part" of Islam be excludable if other parts are not?

Triple Talaq Should Be Considered as One Revocable Talaq and Implied Adjudication

Triple talaq might be considered as one, revocable talaq. It is clear that the practice in most Muslim countries is to treat triple talaq not as three pronouncements in one sitting counting as a valid irrevocable divorce, but rather as one pronouncement. The view that triple talaq cannot be an effective divorce if made as three irrevocable pronouncements in one sitting is supported by many judicial rulings over many decades, and as recently as 2008. This is the correct view and the view that is consonant with the letter and spirit of the Holy Quran, as is clear from many judicial pronouncements and commentary from respected religious leaders/imams.

There is another important way of looking at the issue. In the case of single talaq, although it is revocable from the point of view of the husband, for the wife, it is final subject to the waiting or iddat period. It must be noted that if the husband revokes the talaq, the wife has no option but to return to him. Surely, this is no less onerous for the wife than being divorced instantaneously. However, there is some material to the effect that revocation of the second divorce is possible only with the wife's consent.

The real problem is neither triple talaq nor talaq but the fact that the institutional arrangement of adjudication has been bypassed. Since even the unilateral talaq by the husband has to be for a reasonable cause and preceded by attempts by mediators or arbiters from either side who report to a qazi there is an element of adjudication. Furthermore, the qazi ensures that mehar has been paid and provision made for iddat period (maintenance and residence for the divorced wife) as well as for children before the talaq becomes effective. With intervention of adjudication, all doubts about lack of witnesses and use of modern-day communications like SMS or WhatsApp will be addressed. In any case, no reliable data is forthcoming to show that talaq/triple talaq amongst Muslims exceeds divorce amongst other communities. A recent survey[9] done by Abusaleh Sharif is interesting in this regard, in that it found that only "0.3% divorces occurred due to Oral Instant Triple Talaq in one Go" and that "out of 331 talaqs only one instance has been reported as a clear case of Triple Talaq reported by a female respondent". These findings of the survey are far from infallible, but they do show that the "scourge of triple talaq" may be a much smaller issue than its critics and demonisers would have the world believe.

It is not the principle but the lack of adjudication that causes the problem. Unless talaq (only one part of a comprehensive scheme of marriage and divorce) itself is found unacceptable, the anxiety expressed about triple talaq seems misplaced given that there is more than adequate judicial and legislative material to establish that irrespective of the number of times talaq is pronounced at one sitting it will count only as one. Once that is taken as the accepted position there is no further issue about *halala* since talaq *ahsan* allows a fresh nikah in case the same couple wants to get back together.

A word about *halala* and polygamy is necessary here because there is an assumption that they are indefensible. Intention or *niyat* is an important part of any act ordained or permitted by Islam. *Halala* certainly is not a convenient and, on the face, devious device to allow the exploitation of the woman after three divorces. Understandably, it would pose a greater challenge if triple talaq were permissible because in an instant, the woman is divorced and there is no possibility of regretting and doing a fresh nikah without the woman first marrying someone else. There is no actual requirement of the consummation of such a marriage mentioned in the Holy Quran or the Hadith. The point simply was that three divorces in a lifetime were thought to be enough with two opportunities to revoke talaq within the iddat period or even to remarry thereafter. Beyond that, no further opportunity was to be given, or else marriage and divorce would become a parody. However, if the woman were to unfortunately lose her other husband or get divorced again, there was the ultimate relief of getting back to her first husband. With triple talaq gone, it is difficult to imagine that there would be such an eventuality.

The Court Should Be Circumspect in Entering Matters Essentially within the Legislative or Executive Purview

The Court has repeatedly said that it will be circumspect in going into matters that are essentially the purview of legislative or executive policy. However, there are numerous significant exceptions and indeed the instant case is one. It is undoubtedly within the power and duty of the Court to check the uncontrolled exercise of legislative or executive powers. However, in performing that role, the Court should not be eager to subsume the powers it seeks to check. The Court should refrain from legislating afresh in the guise of commenting upon the constitutional validity of Personal Law. The Court should thus refrain from commenting on issues such as the institution of a Uniform Civil Code, which would fall within the ambit of the legislature. Furthermore, growing jurisprudence on Fundamental Rights might require a fresh look at the Directive Principles–Fundamental Rights relationship read harmoniously in *Minerva Mills*[10] and *Waman Rao*[11] in the Justices Krishna Iyer and Bhagwati era. While Indian law had long recognized that courts cannot be constrained from exploring legal issues under the US doctrine of "political questions", that does not mean that the courts will not show self-imposed restraint in view of separation of powers. If the legislature, in its wisdom, seeks to introduce reforms in Personal Law, it shall be open to the Court to test its validity on several grounds as it was pointed out in the judgment of Justice Nariman. However, it should not seek to frame legislative or executive policies in the guise of judicial pronouncements. It is interesting that unlike previous occasions, this time the Court, has eschewed making a Personal Law matter the springboard for nudging Parliament towards the Uniform Civil Code.

I am certain that this case will not draw the blinds on the issue of religious rights, particularly of minority religious populations of the country. But it is at least able to contribute to a better understanding of the issue across social boundaries and make a real contribution to the future of our nation. What is more, it will put into perspective the debate and endeavours for institutional reforms. In the life of a nation there are some constants and many malleable dimensions. We are yet a young nation in modern times although an ancient civilization. For some people, the growth and evolution of our nation might have ended on a particular date in history, just as some Muslims believed that *ijtehad* came to an end several centuries ago. Neither is of course true. And both must continue in order to lend vitality to, and recharge, our composite heritage. India's strength will ultimately come not from its military prowess and economic dynamics, but its innate spiritual and philosophical dimensions. When the history of Indian law is written about or indeed about the growth of our nation, there will hopefully be a mention of the *Shayara Bano* case before the Constitutional Bench.

6

The Judgment[1]

The *Triple Talaq* case has come and gone but the debate just goes on. It is almost as though the case was a just a peg on which to hang a larger agenda. Most people did not miss the symbolism of a multi-faith Bench: a Sikh, a Christian, a Hindu, a Parsi, and a Muslim. Curiously, all justices agreed that triple talaq had no place in our world. The then Chief Justice even observed that multitudes of Muslim women were clamouring for justice and then went on to appeal to political parties to show understanding in giving talaq a quiet burial, although he felt that Parliament should be the high priest. The channels celebrated as never before: one even offered jalebis to a diabetic clergyman not entirely happy with the outcome. Yet, for those celebrating the emancipation of Muslim women, it must have been irksome to see several of them rejoicing in burkas. When a very carefully moderate Law Minister congratulated them, one even asked what he would now do to help her find her delinquent husband and provide for her children! Gender justice and social justice obviously do not stop with the Supreme Court judgment. Oppression and hunger come from many causes and directions. It must be a sobering thought that there is much to be done. If the concern was truly about justice to all (and therefore gender justice), there is no time to rest on laurels.

The then Chief Justice (with whom Justice Nazeer concurred) made an expansive, erudite exposition of Islam and its history and, in the process, emphasized the unique matrimonial system, including the provision of divorce and dissolution of marriage. Many misplaced notions about Shariah were dispelled, as indeed was the excessively wide proposition of the (now former) Attorney General about the need to strike down talaq per se, so that a replacement law could be put in place by Parliament. The then Chief Justice accepted the Attorney General's invitation only to the extent of Parliament interfering with triple talaq. In essence, in the following passages he proclaimed that triple talaq, being a constituent part of Muslim Personal Law, had Constitutional protection:

193. Religion is a matter of faith, and not of logic. It is not open to a court to accept an egalitarian approach, over a practice which constitutes an integral part of religion. The Constitution allows the followers of every religion, to follow their beliefs and religious traditions. The Constitution assures believers of all faiths, that their way of life, is guaranteed, and would not be subjected to any challenge, even though they may seem to others (and even rationalists, practicing the same faith) unacceptable, in today's world and age. The Constitution extends this guarantee, because

faith constitutes the religious consciousness, of the followers. It is this religious consciousness, which binds believers into separate entities. The Constitution endevours to protect and preserve, the beliefs of each of the separate entities, under Article 25.

194. Despite the views expressed by those who challenged the practice of 'talaq-e-biddat', being able to demonstrate that the practice transcends the barriers of constitutional morality (emerging from different provisions of the Constitution), we have found ourselves unable to persuade ourselves, from reaching out in support of the petitioners concerns. We cannot accept the petitioners' claim, because the challenge raised is in respect of an issue of 'personal law' which has constitutional protection.

The then Chief Justice noted, as did other judges, that the Privy Council had upheld the dichotomy of law and theology:

[30] Rashid Ahmad v. Anisa Khatun: AIR 1932 PC 25.

[...]

(iv) The conclusion: The Privy Council, upheld as valid, 'talaq-e-biddat', triple talaq, pronounced by the husband, in the absence and without the knowledge of the wife, even though the husband and wife continued to cohabit for 15 long years thereafter, wherefrom 5 offsprings were born to them.

Certainly it was as extreme a case as it might be. But the case gave the proposition, 'Bad in theology but good in law.'

During the arguments I heard the Chief Justice say more than once, looking towards me, that I had advised caution to the Court on the matter of interpreting religion:

[137] [...] Mr. Salman Khurshid, learned Senior Advocate also cautioned this Court, that it was not its role to determine the true intricacies of faith

[139] Having given our thoughtful consideration on the entirety of the issue, we are persuaded to accept the counsel of Mr. Kapil Sibal and Mr. Salman Khurshid, Senior Advocates. It would be appropriate for us, to refrain from entertaining a determination on the issue in hand, irrespective of the opinion expressed in the four judgments relied upon by learned counsel for the petitioners, and the Quranic verses and 'hadiths' relied upon by the rival parties. We truly do not find ourselves, upto the task. We have chosen this course, because we are satisfied, that the controversy can be finally adjudicated, even in the absence of an answer to the proposition posed in the instant part of the consideration.

It would be fair that I make my position clear. I certainly advised care and caution given the nature of the exercise but did not go the distance on that with Kapil Sibal. If anything, my position, as stated in this book elsewhere, is that the Court rather than the Parliament is better placed to consider matters of religion and that once Parliament legislates, inevitably challenges will be considered by the Court in any case. It is the manner in which the courts have to undertake this unique exercise with the help of research of arguing counsel as well as experts in the field of Islamic *fiqh*.

Be that as it may, the then Chief Justice summed his effort thus:

Conclusions emerging out of the above consideration:

190. The following conclusions emerge from the considerations recorded at I to IX above:

(1) Despite the decision of the Rashid Ahmad case 1 on the subject of 'talaq-e-biddat', by the Privy Council, the issue needs a fresh examination, in view of the subsequent developments in the matter.

(2) All the parties were unanimous, that despite the practice of 'talaq-e-biddat' being considered sinful, it was accepted amongst Sunni Muslims belonging to the Hanafi school, as valid in law, and has been in practice amongst them.
(3) It would not be appropriate for this Court, to record a finding, whether the practice of 'talaq-e-biddat' is, or is not, affirmed by 'hadiths', in view of the enormous contradictions in the 'hadiths', relied upon by the rival parties.
(4) 'Talaq-e-biddat' is integral to the religious denomination of Sunnis belonging to the Hanafi school. The same is a part of their faith, having been followed for more than 1400 years, and as such, has to be accepted as being constituent of their 'personal law'.
(5) The contention of the petitioners, that the questions/ subjects covered by the Muslim Personal Law (Shariat) Application Act, 1937, ceased to be 'personal law', and got transformed into 'statutory law', cannot be accepted, and is accordingly rejected.
(6) 'Talaq-e-biddat', does not violate the parameters expressed in Article 25 of the Constitution. The practice is not contrary to public order, morality and health. The practice also does not violate Articles 14, 15 and 21 of the Constitution, which are limited to State actions alone.
(7) The practice of 'talaq-e-biddat' being a constituent of 'personal law' has a stature equal to other fundamental rights, conferred in Part III of the Constitution. The practice cannot therefore be set aside, on the ground of being violative of the concept of the constitutional morality, through judicial intervention.
(8) Reforms to 'personal law' in India, with reference to socially unacceptable practices in different religions, have come about only by way of legislative intervention. Such legislative intervention is permissible under Articles 25(2) and 44, read with entry 5 of the Concurrent List, contained in the Seventh Schedule of the Constitution. The said

procedure alone need[s] to be followed with reference to the practice of 'talaq-e-biddat', if the same is to be set aside.

(9) International conventions and declarations are of no avail in the present controversy, because the practice of 'talaq-e-biddat', is a component of 'personal law', and has the protection of Article 25 of the Constitution.

The then Chief Justice nevertheless went on to suggest that Parliament pass legislation putting an end to triple talaq and gave a deadline of six months during which, under Article 142, he granted a stay against such pronouncements. Curiously, since the then Chief Justice was the first to read out his judgment, people assumed that to be the effective part. This was of course the Constitutional Bench and therefore regular Benches might be asked to deal with ultimate relief in the matter. Yet one wonders whether it crosssed the minds of the judges that there remains the question of what is to be the fate of the triple talaq cases that have already been brought before the Court. Normally, such pronouncements are prospective and therefore should not impact the talaqs already granted. Even if those courts hold that triple talaq, that is, the pronouncement of talaq three times in an instant, is ultimately to count as only one pronouncement or one talaq, yet with the passage of three months of iddat the talaq given would by now be irrevocable.

The attitude and approach of the government of the day was quite obvious in the following submissions of the Attorney General, recorded by the then Chief Justice in his judgment:

[77] It is also necessary for us to recount an interesting incident that occurred during the course of hearing. The learned Attorney

General having assisted this Court in the manner recounted above, was emphatic that the other procedures available to Muslim men for obtaining divorce, such as, 'talaq-e-ahsan' and 'talaq-e-hasan' were also liable to be declared as unconstitutional, for the same reasons as have been expressed with reference to 'talaq-e-biddat'. In this behalf, the contention advanced was, that just as 'talaq-e-biddat', 'talaq-e-ahsan' and 'talaq-e-hasan' were based on the unilateral will of the husband, neither of these forms of divorce required the availability of a reasonable cause with the husband to divorce his wife, and neither of these needed the knowledge and/or notice of the wife, and in neither of these procedures the knowledge and/or consent of the wife was required. And as such, the other two so-called approved procedures of divorce ('talaq-e-ahsan' and 'talaq-e-hasan') available to Muslim men, it was submitted, were equally arbitrary and unreasonable, as the practice of 'talaq-e-biddat'. [...] It was contended, that the challenge to 'talaq-e-ahsan' and 'talaq-e-hasan' would follow immediately after this Court had rendered its pronouncement with reference to 'talaq-e-biddat'. We have referred to the incident, and considered the necessity to record it, because of the response of the learned Attorney General to a query raised by the Bench. One of us (U.U. Lalit, J.), enquired from the learned Attorney General, that if all the three procedures referred to above, as were available to Muslim men to divorce their wives, were set aside as unconstitutional, Muslim men would be rendered remedy-less in matters of divorce? The learned Attorney General answered the query in the affirmative. But assured the Court, that the Parliament would enact a legislation within no time, laying down grounds on which Muslim men could divorce their wives. We have accordingly recorded the above episode, because it has relevance to the outcome of the present matter.

Interestingly, other than agreeing on the need to end triple talaq, the five justices disagreed in many ways. The then

Chief Justice found triple talaq to be unwholesome, yet a part of the Hanafi school of Sunni law and prevalent in India for 1,400 years. His Lordship went by what counsel for the Board said and therefore missed the point that Islam has not been in India that long. 'Bad in theology, good in law' pronounced by the Privy Council arrested the vast scholarship he expressed in his long judgment. So he took his cue from Islamic countries and proposed that Parliament legislate to abolish triple talaq and froze the 1,400-year-old practice for six months. To arrive at that conclusion, the then Chief Justice leaned upon Article 25 that protects Personal Law as a Fundamental Right.

In this, Justice Kurian Joseph agreed with the then Chief Justice that Personal Law is a Fundamental Right, thus making that view a majority on that issue (then Chief Justice, Justice Nazeer, and Justice Joseph). But he then went on to hold that triple talaq is not part of Shariah and therefore without legal consequences. This approach was an endorsement of a series of High Court judgments, including that of Justice Badar Ahmed (as he then was) in *Masroor Ahmed* and the Supreme Court itself in *Shamim Ara*. In the words of Justice Joseph:

> 206. [...] I wholly agree with the learned Chief Justice that the 1937 Act is not a legislation regulating talaq. Consequently, I respectfully disagree with the stand taken by Nariman, J. that the 1937 Act is a legislation regulating triple talaq and hence, the same can be tested on the anvil of Article 14. However, on the pure question of law that a legislation, be it plenary or subordinate, can be challenged on the ground of arbitrariness, I agree with the illuminating exposition of law by Nariman, J. I am also of the strong view that the Constitutional democracy of India cannot conceive of a legislation which is arbitrary.

225. To freely profess, practice and propagate religion of one's choice is a Fundamental Right guaranteed under the Indian Constitution. That is subject only to the following (1) public order, (2) health, (3) morality and (4) other provisions of Part III dealing with Fundamental Rights. Under Article 25 (2) of the Constitution of India, the State is also granted power to make law in two contingencies notwithstanding the freedom granted under Article 25(1). Article 25 (2) states that 'nothing in this Article shall affect the operation of any existing law or prevent the State from making any law- (a) regulating or restricting any economic, financial, political or other secular activity which may be associated with religious practice; (b) providing for social welfare and reform or the throwing open of Hindu religious institutions of a public character to all classes and sections of Hindus.' Except to the above extent, the freedom of religion under the Constitution of India is absolute and on this point, I am in full agreement with the learned Chief Justice. However, on the statement that triple talaq is an integral part of the religious practice, I respectfully disagree. Merely because a practice has continued for long, that by itself cannot make it valid if it has been expressly declared to be impermissible. The whole purpose of the 1937 Act was to declare Shariat as the rule of decision and to discontinue anti-Shariat practices with respect to subjects enumerated in Section 2 which include talaq. Therefore, in any case, after the introduction of the 1937 Act, no practice against the tenets of Quran is permissible. Hence, there cannot be any Constitutional protection to such a practice and thus, my disagreement with the learned Chief Justice for the constitutional protection given to triple talaq. I also have serious doubts as to whether, even under Article 142, the exercise of a Fundamental Right can be injuncted.

Justice Kurien Joseph, as indeed the other judges, returned to the question of whether bad in theology can be good in law, as has been the view taken by a series of judgments since the Privy Council first endorsed that view. My response was that it might just be possible in general but certainly not when the Court is interpreting religious law itself. Many analogies have been attempted, including the void or voidable dichotomy in administrative law, but the fact remains that a sin cannot possibly have any degree of validity in the eyes of law in applying theological reasoning.

In a sense, Justice Nariman (with whom Justice Lalit concurred) disagreed with both sides but provided the crucial majority with Justice Lalit and Justice Joseph in striking down triple talaq as violative of the Fundamental Rights chapter of the Constitution. In other words, His Lordship first held that triple talaq was a part of Shariah, and then struck it down on violation of Article 14. But interestingly, Justice Nariman also noted nikah as an 'astonishingly modern' concept, thus giving the self-proclaimed modernist lobby of uniform code advocates something to think about.

Justice Nariman's analysis was quite different from that of Chief Justice Khehar, as His Lordship then was, and Justice Joseph and therefore reached a different conclusion except that he too exorcised triple talaq from the system:

230. [...] The neat question that arises before this Court is, therefore, whether the 1937 Act can be said to recognize and enforce Triple Talaq as a rule of law to be followed by the Courts in India and if not whether Narasu Appa (supra) which states that personal laws are outside Article 13(1) of the Constitution is correct in law.

[...]

235. Marriage in Islam is a contract, and like other contracts, may under certain circumstances, be terminated. There is something

astonishingly modern about this – no public declaration is a condition precedent to the validity of a Muslim marriage nor is any religious ceremony deemed absolutely essential, though they are usually carried out. [...] Prophet Mahomed had declared divorce to be the most disliked of lawful things in the sight of God. The reason for this is not far to seek. Divorce breaks the marital tie which is fundamental to family life in Islam. Not only does it disrupt the marital tie between man and woman, but it has severe psychological and other repercussions on the children from such marriage.

[...]

239. [...] Section 2 of the 1937 Act states:

> 2. Application of Personal law to Muslims. - Notwithstanding any custom or usage to the contrary, in all questions (save questions relating to agricultural land) regarding intestate succession, special property of females, including personal properly inherited or obtained under contract or gift or any other provision of Personal Law, marriage, dissolution of marriage, including talaq, ila, zihar, lian, khula and mubaraat, maintenance, dower, guardianship, gifts, trusts and trust properties, and wakfs (other than charities and charitable institutions and charitable and religious endowments) the rule of decision in cases where the parties are Muslims shall be the Muslim Personal Law (Shariat).

[...]

241. It can be seen that the 1937 Act is a pre-constitutional legislative measure which would fall directly within Article 13(1) of the Constitution of India [...]

242. [...] learned Counsel for the Muslim Personal Board as well as other counsel supporting their stand have argued that, read in light of the Objects and Reasons, the 1937 Act was not meant to enforce Muslim personal law, which was enforceable by itself

through the Courts in India. The 1937 Act was only meant, as the non-obstante clause in Section 2 indicates, to do away with custom or usage which is contrary to Muslim personal law.

[...]

245. It is, therefore, clear that all forms of Talaq recognized and enforced by Muslim personal law are recognized and enforced by the 1937 Act. This would necessarily include Triple Talaq when it comes to the Muslim personal law applicable to Sunnis in India.

[...]

248. It is thus clear that it is this view of the law which the 1937 Act both recognizes and enforces so as to come within the purview of Article 13(1) of the Constitution.

[...]

251. [...] But one important caveat has been entered by this Court, namely, that only what is an essential religious practice is protected under Article 25. A few decisions have laid down what constitutes an essential religious practice.

[...]

And in *Commissioner of Police and Others v. Acharya Jagdishwarananda Avadhuta*,[2] it was stated as under:

> 9. [...] Test to determine whether a part or practice is essential to a religion is to find out whether the nature of the religion will be changed without that part or practice. If the taking away of that part or practice could result in a fundamental change in the character of that religion or in its belief, then such part could be treated as an essential or integral part.

252. Applying the aforesaid tests, it is clear that Triple Talaq is only a form of Talaq which is permissible in law, but at the same time, stated to be sinful by the very Hanafi school which tolerates it.

According to Javed (supra), therefore, this would not form part of any essential religious practice. Applying the test stated in Acharya Jagdishwarananda (supra), it is equally clear that the fundamental nature of the Islamic religion, as seen through an Indian Sunni Muslim's eyes, will not change without this practice. Indeed, Islam divides all human action into five kinds, as has been stated by Hidayatullah, J in his introduction to Mulla. [...]

[...] We have already seen that though permissible in Hanafi jurisprudence, yet, that very jurisprudence castigates Triple Talaq as being sinful. It is clear, therefore, that Triple Talaq forms no part of Article 25(1). This being the case, the submission on behalf of the Muslim Personal Board that the ball must be bounced back to the legislature does not at all arise in that Article 25(2)(b) would only apply if a particular religious practice is first covered under Article 25(1) of the Constitution.

Once Justice Nariman found that triple talaq was incorporated in the general law under Article 13 and did not have the protection of Article 25, it was a foregone conclusion as to how he would deal with it through the lens of other articles of Chapter III of the Constitution. His Lordship proceeded to examine the extensive jurisprudence on equality and reasonableness to find the practice violative and therefore struck down:

282. [...] Manifest arbitrariness, therefore, must be something done by the legislature capriciously, irrationally and/or without adequate determining principle. Also, when something is done which is excessive and disproportionate, such legislation would be manifestly arbitrary. We are, therefore, of the view that arbitrariness in the sense of manifest arbitrariness as pointed out by us above would apply to negate legislation as well under Article 14.

283. Applying the test of manifest arbitrariness to the case at hand, it is clear that Triple Talaq is a form of Talaq which is itself

considered to be something innovative, namely, that it is not in the Sunna, being an irregular or heretical form of Talaq.

The judgment has not entirely cleared the mist, though. Many votaries of the Uniform Civil Code see it as clearing the path for what one channel called 'One Nation, One Law'. But have they purposely overlooked the majority of three Justices giving a clear verdict on protection of Personal Law? A Uniform Civil Code, although mandated by the Directive Principles of State Policy, would still need to pass muster as far as the chapter on Fundamental Rights is concerned. The recent unanimous pronouncement of a Constitutional Bench of nine judges[3] has rearranged the landscape somewhat dramatically and finally laid to rest any doubts about the stand-alone nature of Fundamental Rights and making Article 21 the ultimate repository of rights that people have; indeed, even going further to hold that some rights can be traced to pre-constitutional natural rights. Jurisprudence on Fundamental Rights is a seamless whole and any dent to any part of it will inevitably impact the rest. We made a mistake on civil liberty in the early years of our Independence by subjugating individual rights to the welfare of society in a utilitarian calculus. The result was the Fundamental Rights judgment of the Emergency period[4] that most of the present votaries of the Uniform Civil Code deprecate and indeed, was regretted in later life by the Justices who pronounced it. Furthermore, Justice Nariman's observation on *Nikah*[5] should be a warning that the Uniform Code will certainly not be a majoritarian version of what is desirable. For instance, not one person has ever ventured to explore whether a Uniform Code will require that all funerals culminate in a similar manner, that is, would everyone be cremated, buried, or confined to the Towers of Silence? Furthermore, under the marriage provisions, would same-sex marriages be permitted as they now are in a growing number of countries across the globe?

The judgment certainly gives clues to what might be the final outcome of pending proceedings in the Section 377 *Naz Foundation*[6] matter, but that would go only to the extent of decriminalization of same-sex consensual relationships. Modernism might not be as simple as some people make it out to be in order to promote petty political aspirations. The misplaced belief that modernizing community law is essentially a matter of reviewing different religious practices from the point of view of a version assumed to be superior is destructive to the notion of diversity that is a cornerstone of our democracy. Besides the philosophical dimension, there is also the political reality of diverse sub-cultures. How much of tribal culture should be preserved in the face of modernity is far from a settled question of our democracy. Modes of marriage vary vastly in different parts of the country, particularly with matriarchal societies in certain parts. It might be possible to let a universal idea of equality prevail in the matter of genders by a degree of interference with existing systems, but then where would one draw a line of balance? People who question the right of human beings to sacrifice animals for religious reasons (because they are vegetarians or subscribe to non-violence as a matter of faith)[7] might end up having to question *bali* for Hindu Goddesses as much as the *qurbani* rituals of Muslims.

An interesting point was raised in a tweet by my erudite colleague, Shri P. Chidambaram, after the judgment was delivered. He tweeted that only triple talaq (meaning the instant talaq) has been declared unlawful and that other forms of talaq remain to be considered, being equally unilateral. The Attorney General had made similar arguments during the hearing. Then again, another colleague has been reported to have opined that Parliament still has a role to play to implement the judgment. These raise much wider questions far beyond triple talaq. Even the Supreme Court did not envisage going that far and simply indicated that nikah halala and polygamy would be considered by another Bench in due course. As to why the concept of talaq does not suffer from the mischief of triple talaq, the answer is to be found in the remarkably erudite exposition of Shariah by the then Chief Justice. As far as the intervention of Parliament is concerned, it is surprising that a matter that the majority of the Supreme Court steered clear of—not because it found it expedient and appropriate, but because it did not see the jurisprudential ground for passing the buck to Parliament—should be assumed by some persons as a signal to Parliament to proceed. Thus any attempt by Parliament to venture into this area will inevitably come back to the Supreme Court, where a later generation of judges will have to look for guidance in the present judgment of the Constitutional Bench. Hopefully, the myopic concession of the Board, that although the Court cannot interfere in the matter yet Parliament can legislate to obliterate a 1,400-year-old matter of faith will not restrict their options. Ultimately, the Court will have to decide if equality is uniformity or diversity too is desirable. Triple talaq was obviously not a deserving test for that proposition because of its inherent odious nature and its questionable pedigree.

It is, indeed, important that we retain a rational perspective on the entire affair, keeping our sights focused on the then Chief Justice's beacon—that rationality and faith cannot be tested against each other but must instead be kept in a careful balance in our society. Barely days after the Supreme Court judgment came the verdict in the prolonged trial of Baba Gurmeet Ram Rahim of Dera Sacha Sauda. The mayhem that was unleashed by his devotees, as indeed the dark stories that came tumbling out in the media, were a sharp reminder that the rule of law, based essentially on reason, has great challenges in the hysteria of the faithful. The age of reason still has a long way to go before it can be said to be universally accepted in our land where the cults of modern-day demi-gods continue to spread their tentacles and political leaders, too, are generously borrowing from their style and substance. Morality seems under threat from a combination of a return to the past and rushing towards postmodern, permissive social mores. Shiv Visvanathan,[8] an outstanding sociologist eloquently describes the modern-day predicament of our democracy:

> We have two options: dismiss Ram Rahim Singh as a law and order problem or go out and understand what is happening to our culture today under the stress of modernity and globalization. The proliferation of goddesses, the epidemic of gurus, and the appeal of millennialism reveals that India is a mix of secularism, faith, and superstition that has an experimental pluralist quality to it. It demands that we step out of our drawing-room ideas of governance and social science and get a vernacular sense of what India is thinking beyond the realm of consumption and marketing today.

For people who believe that India's problems arise from the backward mentality of its Muslim population (as though Pakistan does not have any problems!), the judgment came as a vindication of their unsuccessful battle in *Shah Bano* some thirty years ago. Arif Mohammed Khan, who resigned from the Congress government to lead that battle, certainly did not shy away from receiving bouquets. Yet, to place *Shayara Bano* in the same category as *Shah Bano* is either a mistake or mischief—plain and simple. We must not allow the result of a proposition to be confused with the legitimacy of the argument. What is instinctively desirable may well not be sound in terms of the agreed rules of engagement, and any attempt to cut corners might lead to unintended consequences. Thus, the former is about understanding what Islam and Shariah ordain, while *Shah Bano* was about the general law being used to interfere with the outcome of Shariah. A brief diversion would be useful here, given that people confidently pronounce on the regressive nature of Parliamentary interference by way of the passage of the Protection of Women (on divorce) Act, 1976.

Shah Bano was given talaq by her husband after many years of marriage. She claimed maintenance under Section 125 of the CrPC before a Magistrate. The maximum she could have been granted was Rs 500, but the actual amount directed to be paid was a paltry sum of Rs 159. The matter travelled to the Supreme Court. Her husband argued in Court—as indeed a large number argued in the streets—that a talaq brings to an end what is essentially a contract of marriage on its own terms and thereafter there can be no direct or indirect relationship between the erstwhile spouses. Asking a former husband to pay a maintenance amount every month was seen as bypassing the Shariah. In other words, the Shariah provides a complete code of matrimonial law, and includes the contractual nature of marriage (nikah), the payment of dower (mehar) by the husband as consideration of marriage, the different methods of talaq (with only form being unilateral but with conditions and safeguards), provision and maintenance (*nan-nafqa*) during the compulsory waiting of three months (iddat), right of the woman to the custody of minor children, and so on. By superimposing the provisions for maintenance under Section 125, the Court was seen as overriding the Shariah. It was entirely possible for the Court to have underscored that it had no intention to interfere with the Shariah arrangements as they existed, but was merely adding on assistance to an indigent woman. However, the Court opted to take a reformist angle, going to the extent of advising a fresh look at Uniform Civil Code.

The *Shah Bano* judgment led to a huge outcry from the traditionalists with an equally loud response from the reformists and self-proclaimed progressives. The ruling Congress party was pushed into a no-win quandary and after a feisty debate between Arif Mohammed Khan and Zia-ur-Rehman Ansari, two members of the Council of Ministers, the die was cast in favour of overruling the Supreme Court judgment. Parliament therefore passed the Protection of Muslim Women (on divorce) Bill, 1976 which was unfairly seen as a regressive step but in fact found the right balance between ensuring justice to a divorced woman and putting it in a way that it could not be said to be interfering with the scheme of Shariah. This view finds its validation in the subsequent judgment handed down by five judges in the *Daniel Latifi* constitutional challenge to the legislation. It is interesting that in all the years that have passed since, no one has made any effort to collect data on how the entire episode has impacted the condition of Muslim women. The narrative popularized by some remarkable women who have taken up cudgels for justice unfortunately is taken as vindication of the view that generally Muslim women are an exploited lot and owe their condition to the inherent gender biases in Islam. Nothing could be further from the truth and, in some ways, the *Shayara Bano* judgment corrects that impression though not entirely.

At the time that the dust of the *Shah Bano* controversy was yet to settle, the late Rajiv Gandhi had met with a large delegation of Aligarh Muslim University students. In the discussion that took place it was brought home to the then Prime Minister that no single dimension of a religious or moral code should be seen in isolation. It was the entire scheme that needed to be considered. Rajiv Gandhi grasped the point quickly and said, 'I understand we must accept the way of life perceived by each community for its members'. That indeed is the essence of diversity that we celebrate in our democracy. What we need to deal with are occasions when one way of life is said to interfere with another way of life. But that is central to all differences in liberal societies. An individual cannot complain about another person's conduct unless it directly or indirectly prevents her from doing something she wishes to.

Quick upon the heels of *Shayara Bano* came the historical 9 Bench *Privacy* judgment,[9] which has widened the scope of Fundamental Rights far beyond their previously assumed contours. Given that clear indications are available that many attributes of personal life are protected in the expanded version of privacy and personal dignity, the Court's finding that Personal Law is a Fundamental Right opens up vast avenues for the future. The emphasis on an individual's autonomy, the Right to be Left Alone, and the concept of pre-constitutional rights being natural rights pose the challenge of how we will, henceforth, treat something that we dislike or find offensive. The Constitutional Bench gave pretty clear hints about the fate of the famous *Naz Foundation* judgment[10] under review, although the actual outcome would be known only once that matter is taken up for hearing. However, one can safely cite Chief Justice A.P. Shah's (as His Lordship then was) following paragraph from the Delhi High Court judgment in support of Personal law,[11] although at the time, Muslim clergy had opposed the outcome:

131. Where society can display inclusiveness and understanding, such persons can be assured of a life of dignity and non-discrimination. This was the 'spirit behind the Resolution' of which Nehru spoke so passionately. In our view, Indian Constitutional law does not permit the statutory criminal law to be held captive by the popular misconceptions of who the LGBTs are. It cannot be forgotten that discrimination is anti-thesis of equality and that it is the recognition of equality which will foster the dignity of every individual.

As I mentioned before, towards the end of arguments in the matter, the Board seems to have resiled from its rigid position and filed an affidavit recording their intent for future. The then Chief Justice took note of the affidavit in arriving at the view that the matter was appropriate for Parliament to handle the petitioners' challenge. The affidavit affirmed the following position:[12]

2. [T]he All India Muslim Personal Board will issue an advisory through its Website, Publications and Social Media Platforms and

thereby advise the persons who perform 'Nikah' (marriage) and request them to do the following:

(a) At the time of performing 'Nikah' (marriage), the person performing the 'Nikah' will advise the Bridegroom/Man that in case of differences leading to Talaq the Bridegroom/Man shall not pronounce three divorces in one sitting since it is an undesirable practice in Shariat;
(b) That at the time of performing 'Nikah' (Marriage), the person performing the 'Nikah' will advise both the Bridegroom/Man and the Bride/Woman to incorporate a condition in the 'Nikahnama' to exclude resorting to pronouncement of three divorces by her husband in one sitting.

3. I say and submit that, in addition, the Board is placing on record, that the Working Committee of the Board had earlier already passed certain resolutions in the meeting held on 15th & 16th April, 2017 in relation to Divorce (Talaq) in the Muslim community. Thereby it was resolved to convey a code of conduct/guidelines to be followed in the matters of divorce particularly emphasizing to avoid pronouncement of three divorces in one sitting."

Despite the affidavit, members of the Board did not respond in unison once the judgment was pronounced. Their counsel, Kapil Sibal, welcomed it in a special press briefing and some members joined him in applauding the Court in granting Personal Law the status of a Fundamental Right. Some voices, however, rejected the judgment as interference with Islam and publicly wondered how it would be implemented. There were public assertions of intent to collect lakhs of signatures from Muslim women in support of triple talaq. On the other hand, Indira Jaising spoke of the need to give Hindu women the right of a contract of marriage as well as further steps towards the

Uniform Civil Code. Clearly, there are many different ways in which the judgment is being read and understood.

It is interesting that the Board, as indeed Muslim scholars, seldom attempt to explain that Islam is followed in India in a unique manner, in that the criminal dimension of Shariah has never been applied and many practices are made subject to the general law of the land without any protest from Muslims. Although polygamy remains lawful (subject, of course, to strict conditions), government regulations prohibiting polygamy for civil servants has quietly been accepted by Muslims. Similarly, restrictions on cow slaughter have been widely accepted across the country. It is another matter that the Supreme Court has not upheld the ban on the footing of faith and made strenuous efforts to justify it on the Directive Principles ground of agriculture.[13]

Furthermore, in interpreting or applying Shariah, there has been little inclination to open the Pandora's box of conflict of laws given that the four schools of Shariah differ on important aspects, as indeed Hanafi and Maliki do on triple talaq. It seems that there are no rules to decide whether the rule of reason to be applied in the case of parties of different schools would weigh in favour of the maslaq of the plaintiff or the defendant. The Muslim Marriage Dissolution Act, 1939 attempted such an exercise.

The essence of Islam as understood over the centuries—including in the syncretic flavour in India with the merging of the Bhakti movement and Sufism—has sadly been overtaken by the recent growth of political Islam across the world, often mistakenly described as jihadist Islam. How grievously wrong that description is (of Islam, not of those who purport to use it for the wrong reasons) and how much irreparable damage that has done to Islam is unimaginable. Fortunately, Osama bin Laden is no hero for young Muslims in India as Yasser Arafat, Gamal Abdul Nasser, Kemal Atatürk, and Saddam Hussein once were (as they indeed were for all Indians). Sadly, however, the draw of the ideology of Frontier Gandhi, Khan Abdul Gaffar Khan, has receded into a hazy past as violence rules. Even in the Kashmir Valley, attempts to remind young people of their Kashmiriyat heritage falls on deaf ears or is lost in the din of Aazadi slogans. In an age of iconic pseudo-spiritual and political leaders, there is a desperate need for statesmen and social healers. To calm the decibel of disagreement, we need a voice of reason and compassion. The right to dissent must not be overwhelmed by proclivity for defiance.

Although the large question of reform and assimilation of the Shariah will continue to be debated for a while, it is important to keep in mind that historically there has been no demand that the criminal law, at least for Muslims, be in accordance with the Shariah. Strictly speaking, Islamic law does not have a distinct corpus of criminal law. Crimes are treated in three categories depending on the nature of the offence—*hudud* for crimes "against God", whose punishment is fixed in the Quran and the Hadith); *qisa*s for crimes against an individual or family whose punishment is equal retaliation in the Quran and the Hadith, but even in matter of unlawful death, the victim's family has the option of seeking compensation instead of execution; and *tazir* for crimes whose punishment is not specified in the Holy Quran and the Hadith, and is left to the discretion of the ruler or qazi. Crimes against God are prosecuted by the State as hudud crimes, and all other criminal matters, including murder and bodily injury, are treated as disputes between individuals. The offences incurring hudud punishments are *zina* (unlawful sexual intercourse), unfounded accusations of zina, consuming intoxicants, highway robbery, and some forms of theft. Such crimes cannot be pardoned by the victim or by the State. The punishments must be carried out in public and include lashings, stoning to death, amputation of hands, and crucifixion. However, the evidentiary standards for these punishments were often impossibly high, and they were infrequently implemented. For example, meeting hudud requirements for zina and theft was virtually impossible without a confession, which could be invalidated by a retraction. Based on a Hadith, jurists stipulated that hudud punishments should be averted by the slightest doubts or ambiguities. In the nineteenth century, legislation replaced Shariah and harsh punishments in most parts of the world. All we hear from time to time are conservative demands in Islamic countries like Pakistan and Malaysia for a return to Shariah. In India, there is no record of any similar demand in recent centuries. When pressed, Islamic scholars speak of strict compliance being necessary in purely Islamic countries. In that sense there are several matters in which accommodation has been made from time to time to adjust with ground realities, such as the willingness of Muslims to abjure beef in vast parts of India, their acceptance of the strict requirement of monogamy for State sector employment, and not insisting on extra time off from normal duties for Friday prayers. There are, of course, periodic disagreements that seem more because of political assertion than for pure religious concerns, such as the demand for prayers in historical mosques in the custody of the Archaeological Survey of India (ASI). Fortunately,

India can be cited as a pristine example of plural existence. For this to have happened, rulers and theologians over the centuries have shown remarkable innovative spirit to ensure harmonious existence in the spirit of the Surat Al-Kafirun[14]: *"lakum dinakum, waliadin"* ("to you, your religion, to me, mine"). In India, we often encapsulate that in *"sarv dharm sambhaav"*. One might ask if the real essence of peaceful coexistence does not lie in that principle. The Court has interfered with the right of Hindu women to access the sanctum sanctorum of religious places of worship as indeed of Muslim women to enter the *mazar* of Haji Ali in Mumbai, but would it as easily interfere with the Akal Takht[15] declaring some one *tankhiya* (guilty of religious misconduct)? Although the Court, in recent times, has crafted ways to combine public law remedies for private conflicts that have larger public implications—as in the present case—the distinction remains intact under Articles 12 and 13. In that sense, Parliament has greater freedom to interfere subject to judicial scrutiny.

Ultimately we need to ask ourselves the question if social groups based on religion or community have an autonomous existence, to a certain extent, in the larger Indian society, which has been described variously as a rainbow or a mosaic? Alternatively, they are all like the Princely States at the time of Independence that lost their separate identity by merging into the Indian nation. But while the Constitution made provisions such as Article 370 in the case of former, for the latter, Articles 25 to 30 provide much greater protection. But this often is lost sight of in formulating a superficial understanding of Indian unity.

7

Triple Talaq Judgment Excerpts[I]

Till now, I have sought to give you a glimpse of the work that went into this landmark judgment, the roles of some of the players, and some accounts based on my own journey through the literature and opinion around Islam and triple talaq. However, sometimes it is best to hear it "from the horse's mouth".

To that intent, I have included in this chapter excerpts from the three judgments that came down in the case of *Shayara Bano v. Union of India*, each concurring and dissenting with the others in part. A judgment such as the one that came down in this case can be a challenge to understand—often because its language is a mix of legalism and philosophy, and also because its true impact may yet be years in the offing. But to make the task somewhat easier, I have chosen excerpts that have been particularly helpful to me in writing this book. At the risk of some repetition, I reproduce them for you below, in the exact words of the judges that presided over this landmark case, and in the exact way in which they chose to present them.

* * *

Chief Justice J.S. Khehar (Justice Nazeer Concurring)

11. [...] Talaq understood simply, is a means of divorce, at the instance of the husband. 'Khula', is another mode of divorce, this divorce is at the instance of the wife. The third category of divorce is 'mubaraat' – divorce by mutual consent.

16. [...] It was however emphasized, that even those schools that recognized 'talaq-e-biddat' described it, "as a sinful form of divorce". It is acknowledged, that this form of divorce, has been described as "bad in theology, but good in law". We have recorded the instant position at this juncture, because learned Counsel for the rival parties, uniformly acknowledge the same.

[18] During the course of hearing, references to the Quran were made from 'The Holy Quran: Text Translation and Commentary' by Abdullah Yusuf Ali (published by Kitab Bhawan, New Delhi, 14th edition, 2016). Learned counsel representing the rival parties commended, that the text and translation in this book, being the most reliable, could safely be relied upon.

[...]

To prevent erratic and fitful repeated separations and reunions, a limit of two divorces is prescribed. In other words, reconciliation after two divorces is allowed. After the second divorce, the parties must definitely make up their mind, either to dissolve their ties permanently, or to live together honourably, in mutual love and forbearance—to hold together on equitable terms. [...] After the divorce, a husband cannot seek the return of gifts or properties, he may have given to his wife. Such retention by the wife is permitted, only in recognition that the wife is economically weaker. An exception has been carved out in the second part of 'verse' 229, that in situations where the freedom of the wife could suffer on account of the husband refusing to dissolve the marriage, and perhaps, also treat her with cruelty. It is permissible for the wife, in such a situation, to extend some material consideration to the husband. Separation of this kind, at the instance of the wife, is called 'khula'.

19. [...] 'Verse' 35, sets out the course of settlement of family disputes. It postulates the appointment of two arbitrators – one representing the family of the husband, and the other the family of the wife. The arbitrators are mandated to explore the possibility of reconciliation. In case reconciliation is not possible, dissolution is advised, without publicity or mud-throwing or by resorting to trickery or deception.

22. [...] Muslim women claimed, that the Muslim 'personal law' be made applicable to them. It is therefore, that the Muslim Personal Law (Sharait) Application Act, 1937 (hereinafter referred to, as the Shariat Act), was passed.

23. Sections 2 [...] of the Shariat Act are relevant and are extracted hereunder:

> 2. Application of personal law to Muslims.– Notwithstanding any customs or usage to the contrary, in all questions (save questions relating to agricultural land) regarding intestate succession, special property of females, including personal property inherited or obtained under contract or gift or any other provision of Personal Law, marriage, dissolution of

marriage, including talaq, ila, zihar, lian, khula and mubaraat, maintenance, dower, guardianship, gifts, trusts and trust properties, and wakfs (other than charities and charitable institutions and charitable and religious endowments) the Rule of decision in cases where the parties are Muslims shall be the Muslim Personal Law (Shariat).

[...]

A close examination of Section 2, extracted above, leaves no room for any doubt, that custom and usage, as it existed amongst Muslims, were sought to be expressly done away with, to the extent the same were contrary to Muslim 'personal law'.

24. It is relevant to highlight herein, that under Section 5 of the Shariat Act provided, that a Muslim woman could seek dissolution of her marriage, on the grounds recognized under the Muslim 'personal law'. It would also be relevant to highlight, that Section 5 of the Shariat Act was deleted, and replaced by the Dissolution of Muslim Marriages Act, 1939.

26. The Dissolution of Muslim Marriages Act, 1939 provided, the grounds on which a Muslim woman, could seek dissolution of marriage. Section 2 of the enactment is reproduced below:

2. Grounds for decree for dissolution of marriage.–A woman married under Muslim law shall be entitled to obtain a decree for the dissolution of her marriage on any one or more of the following grounds, namely:
    i. that the whereabouts of the husband have not been known for a period of four years;
    ii. that the husband has neglected or has failed to provide for her maintenance for a period of two years;
    iii. that the husband has been sentenced to imprisonment for a period of seven years or upwards;
    iv. that the husband has failed to perform, without reasonable cause, his marital obligations for a period of three years;

v. that the husband was impotent at the time of the marriage and continues to be so;

vi. that the husband has been insane for a period of two years or is suffering from leprosy or virulent venereal disease;

vii. that she, having been given in marriage by her father or other guardian before she attained the age of fifteen years, repudiated the marriage before attaining the age of eighteen years:

Provided that the marriage has not been consummated;

viii. that the husband treats her with cruelty, that is to say,–

(a) habitually assaults her or makes her life miserable by cruelty of conduct even if such conduct does not amount to physical ill-treatment, or

(b) associates with women of evil repute or leads an infamous life, or

(c) attempts to force her to lead an immoral life, or

(d) disposes of her property or prevents her exercising her legal rights over it, or

(e) obstructs her in the observance of her religious profession or practice, or

(f) if he has more wives than one, does not treat her equitably in accordance with the injunctions of the Quran;

ix. on any other ground which is recognised as valid for the dissolution of marriages under Muslim law:

Provided that–

(a) no decree shall be passed on ground (iii) until the sentence has become final;

(b) a decree passed on ground (i) shall not take effect for a period of six months from the date of such decree, and if the husband appears either in person or through an authorised agent within that period and satisfies the Court that he is prepared to perform his conjugal duties, the Court shall set aside the said decree; and

(c) before passing a decree on ground (v) the Court shall, on application by the husband, make an order requiring the husband to satisfy the Court within a period of one year from the date of such order that he has ceased to be impotent, and if the husband so satisfies the Court within such period, no decree shall be passed on the said ground.

27. [...] [T]he Dissolution of Muslim Marriages Act, 1939, is irrelevant for the present controversy on account of the fact, that the issue in hand does not pertain to the dissolution of marriage at the behest of a Muslim wife (but pertains to the dissolution of marriage, at the behest of a Muslim husband).

28. 'Muslim Law in India and Abroad', by Tahir Mahmood and Saif Mahmood (Universal Law Publishing Co. Pvt. Ltd., New Delhi, 2012 edition), records the following position about the abrogation of the practice of 'talaq-e-biddat' as a means of divorce, through statutory enactments, the world over [...]

A. Laws of Arab States

i. Algeria: Is a theocratic State, which declares Islam to be its official religion. Muslims of the Sunni sect constitute its majority. On the issue in hand, it has enacted the following legislation:

Code of Family Law 1984

Law No. 4–11 of 1984 as amended in 2005

Article 49. Divorce cannot be established except by a judgment of the court, preceded by an attempt at reconciliation for a period not exceeding three months.

ii. Egypt: Is a secular State. Muslims of the Sunni sect constitute its majority. On the issue in hand, it has enacted the following legislation:

Law of Personal Status 1929

Law 25 of 1929 as amended by Law 100 of 1985

Article 1. A Talaq pronounced under the effect of intoxication or compulsion shall not be effective.

Article 2. A conditional Talaq which is not meant to take effect immediately shall have no effect if it is used as an inducement to do some act or to abstain from it.

Article 3. A Talaq accompanied by a number, expressly or impliedly, shall not be effective except as a single revocable divorce.

Article 4. Symbolic expressions of talaq, i.e., words which may or may not bear the implication of a divorce, shall not effect a divorce unless the husband actually intended it.

iii. Iraq: Is a theocratic State, which declares Islam to be its official religion. The majority of Iraq's Muslims is Shias. On the issue in hand, it has enacted the following legislation:

Code of Personal Status 1959

Law 188 of 1959 as amended by Law 90 of 1987

Article 35. No divorce shall be effective when pronounced by the persons mentioned below:

(a) one who is intoxicated, insane or imbecile, under duress, or not in his senses due to anger, sudden calamity, old age or sickness;

(b) a person in death-sickness or in a condition which in all probabilities is fatal and of which he actually dies, survived by his wife.

xxx xxx xxx

Article 37. (1) Where a Talaq is coupled with a number, express or implied, not more than one divorce shall take place.

(2) If a woman is divorced thrice on three separate occasions by her husband, no revocation or remarriage would be permissible after that.

xxx xxx xxx

Article 39. (1) When a person intends to divorce his wife, he shall institute a suit in the Court of Personal Status requesting that it be effected and that an order be issued therefor. If a person cannot so approach the court, registration of the divorce in the court during the period of Iddat shall be binding on him.

(2) The certificate of marriage shall remain valid till it is cancelled by the court.

iv. Jordan: Is a secular State. Muslims of the Sunni sect constitute its majority. On the issue in hand, it has enacted the following legislation:

Code of Personal Status 1976

Law 61 of 1976

Article 88. (1) Talaq shall not be effective if pronounced under intoxication, bewilderment, compulsion, mental disorder, depression or effect of sleep.

(2) 'Bewildered' is one who has lost senses due to anger or provocation, etc., and cannot understand what he is saying.

xxx xxx xxx

Article 90. A divorce coupled with a number, expressly or impliedly, as also a divorce repeated in the same sitting, will not take effect except as asingle divorce.

xxx xxx xxx

Article 94. Every divorce shall be revocable except the final third, onebefore consummation and one with consideration.

xxx xxx xxx

Article 98. Where an irrevocable Talaq was pronounced once or twice, renewal of marriage with the consent of parties is not prohibited.

v. Kuwait: Is a theocratic State, which declares Islam to be the official religion. Muslims of the Sunni sect constitute its majority. On the issue in hand, it has the following legislation in place:

Code of Personal Status 1984

Law 51 of 1984

Article 102. Talaq may be effected by major and sane men acting by their free will and understanding the implications of their action. Therefore Talaq shall not take effect if the husband is mentally handicapped, imbecile, under coercion, mistake, intoxication, fear or high anger affecting his speech and action.

xxx xxx xxx

Article 109. If a Talaq is pronounced with a number (two, three) by words, signs or writing, only one Talaq shall take effect.

vi. Lebanon: Is a secular State. Muslims constitute its majority, which is estimated to be 54% (27% Shia, and 27% Sunni). On the issue in hand, it has enacted the following legislation:

Family Rights Law 1962

Law of 16 July 1962

Article 104. A divorce by a drunk person shall have no effect.

Article 105. A divorce pronounced under coercion shall have no effect.

vii. Libya: Is a theocratic State, which declares Islam to be its official religion. Muslims of the Sunni sect constitute its majority. On the issue in hand, it has enacted the following legislation:

Family Law 1984

Law 10 of 1984 as amended by Law 15 of 1984

Article 28. Divorce is termination of the marriage bond. No divorce will become effective in any case except by a decree of a competent court and subject to the provision of Article 30.

Article 29. Divorce is of two kinds – revocable and irrevocable. Revocable divorce does not terminate the marriage till the expiry of Iddat.

Irrevocable divorce terminates the marriage forthwith.

Article 30. All divorces shall be revocable except a third-time divorce, one before consummation of marriage, one for a consideration, and those specified in this law to be irrevocable.

Article 31. A divorce shall be effective only if pronounced in clear words showing intention to dissolve the marriage. Symbolic or metaphorical expression will not dissolve the marriage.

Article 32. A divorce pronounced by a minor or insane person, or if pronounced under coercion, or with no clear intention to dissolve the marriage, shall have no legal effect.

Article 33. (1) A divorce meant to be effect on some action or omission of the wife shall have no legal effect.

(2) A divorce given with a view to binding the wife to an oath or restrain her from doing something shall have no legal effect.

(3) A divorce to which a number is attached, by express words or a gesture, shall effect only a single revocable divorce, except when it is pronounced for the third time.

xxx xxx xxx

Article 35. The marriage may be dissolved by mutual consent of the parties. Such a divorce must be registered with the court. If the parties cannot agree on the terms of such a divorce, they shall approach the court and it will appoint arbitrators to settle the matter or reconcile them.

xxx xxx xxx

Article 47. A divorce must be pronounced in a court and in the presence of the other party or his or her representative. The court shall before giving effect to a divorce exhaust all possibilities of reconciliation.

viii. Morocco: Is a theocratic State, which declares Islam to be its official religion. Muslims of the Sunni sect constitute its majority. On the issue in hand, it has enacted the following legislation:

Code of Personal Status 2004

Law 70.03 of 2004

Article 79. Whoever divorces his wife by Talaq must petition the court for permission to register it with the Public Notaries of the area where the matrimonial home is situate[d], or where the wife resides, or where the marriage took place.

Article 80. The petition will mention the identity of spouses, their professions, addresses, number of children, if any, with their age, health condition and educational status. It must be supported by a copy of the marriage agreement and a document stating the husband's social status and financial obligations.

Article 81. The court shall summon the spouses and attempt reconciliation. If the husband deliberately abstains, this will be deemed to be withdrawal of the petition. If the wife abstains, the court will notify her that if she does not present herself the petition may be decided in her absence. If the husband has fraudulently given a wrong address for the wife, he may be prosecuted at her instance.

Article 82. The court will hear the parties and their witnesses in camera and take all possible steps to reconcile them, including appointment of arbitrators or a family reconciliation council, and if there are children such efforts shall be exhausted within thirty days. If reconciliation takes place, a report will be filed with the court.

Article 83. If reconciliation attempts fail, the court shall fix an amount to be deposited by the husband in the court within thirty days towards payment of the wife's post-divorce dues and maintenance of children.

xxx xxx xxx

Article 90. No divorce is permissible for a person who is not in his senses or is under coercion or provocation.

xxx xxx xxx

Article 92. Multiple expressions of divorce, oral or written, shall have the effect of a single divorce only.

xxx xxx xxx

Article 123. Every divorce pronounced by the husband shall be revocable, except a third-time divorce, divorce before consummation of marriage, divorce by mutual consent, and divorce by Khula or Talaq-e-Tafweez.

ix. Sudan: Is a theocratic State, which declares Islam to be its official religion. Muslims of the Sunni sect constitute its majority. On the issue in hand, it has the following legislation in place:

Law on Talaq 1935

Judicial Proclamation No.4 of 1935

Article 1. A divorce uttered in a state of intoxication or under duress shall be invalid and ineffective.

Article 2. A contingent divorce which is not meant to be effective immediately and is used as an inducement or threat shall have not effect.

Article 3. A formula of divorce coupled with a number, expressly or impliedly, shall effect only one divorce.

Article 4. Metaphorical expressions used for a divorce shall have the effect of dissolving the marriage only if the husband actually meant a divorce.

x. Syria: Is a secular State. Muslims of the Sunni sect constitute its majority. On the issue in hand, it has enacted the following legislation:

Code of Personal Status 1953

Law 59 of 1953 as amended by Law 34 of 1975

Article 89. No divorce shall take place when the man is drunk, out of his senses, or under duress. A person is out of his senses when due to anger, etc. he does not appreciate what he says.

Article 90. A conditional divorce shall have no effect if not actually intended and used only as an inducement to do or abstain from doing something or as an oath or persuasion.

xxx xxx xxx

Article 92. If a divorce is coupled with a number, expressly or impliedly, not more than one divorce shall take place.

xxx xxx xxx

Article 94. Every divorce shall be revocable except a third-time divorce, one before consummation, a divorce with a consideration, and a divorce stated in this Code to be irrevocable.

xxx xxx xxx

Article 117. Where a person divorces his wife the court may, if satisfied that he has arbitrarily done so without any reasonable cause and that as a result of the divorce the wife shall suffer damage and become destitute, give a decision, with due regard to the husband's financial condition and the amount of wife's suffering, that he should pay her compensation not exceeding three years' maintenance, in addition to maintenance payable during the period of Iddat. It may be directed to be paid either in a lump sum or in instalments as the circumstances of a case may require.

xi. Tunisia: Is a theocratic State, which declares Islam to be its official religion. Muslims of the Sunni sect constitute its majority. On the issue in hand, it has enacted the following legislation:

Code of Personal Status 1956

Law 13–8 of 1956 as amended by Law 7 of 1981

Article 31. (1) A decree of divorce shall be given: (i) with the mutual consent of the parties; or (ii) at the instance of either party on the ground of injury; or (iii) if the husband insists on divorce or the wife demands it. The party causing material or mental injury by the fact of divorce under clauses (ii) and (iii) shall be directed to indemnify the aggrieved spouse.

(2) As regards the woman to be indemnified for material injury in terms of money, the same shall be paid to her after the expiry of Iddat and may be in the form of retention of the matrimonial home. This indemnity will be subject to revision, increase or decrease in accordance with the changes in the circumstances of the divorced wife until she is alive or until she changes her marital status by marrying again. If the former husband dies, this indemnity will be a charge on his estate and will have to be met by his heirs if they consent to it

and will be decided by the court if they disagree. They may pay her in a lump sum within one year from the former husband's death the indemnity claimable by her.

Article 32. (1) No divorce shall be decreed except after the court has made an overall inquiry into the causes of rift and failed to effect reconciliation.

(2) Where no reconciliation is possible the court shall provide, even if not asked to, for all important matters relating to the residence of the spouses, maintenance and custody of children and meeting the children, except when the parties specifically agree to forgo all or any of these rights. The court shall fix the maintenance on the basis of all those facts which it comes to know while attempting reconciliation. All important matters shall be provided for in the decree, which shall be non-appealable but can be reviewed for making additional provisions.

(3) The court of first instance shall pass orders in the matters of divorce and all concerning matters including the compensation money to which the divorced wife may be entitled after the expiry of Iddat. The portions of the decree relating to custody, maintenance, compensation, residence and right to visit children shall be executed immediately.

xii. United Arab Emirates: Is a theocratic State, as the Federal Constitution declares Islam to be the official religion. The Constitution also provides for freedom of religion, in accordance with established customs. Muslims of the Shia sect constitute its majority. On the issue in hand, it has the following legislation in place:
Law of Personal Status 2005
Federal Law No. 28 of 2005

Article 140(1) If a husband divorces his wife after consummation of a valid marriage by his unilateral action and without any move for divorce from her side, she will be entitled to compensation besides maintenance for Iddat. The amount of compensation will be decided with due regard to the means of the husband and the hardship suffered by the wife, but it shall not exceed the amount of one year's maintenance payable in law to a woman of her status.

(2) The Kazi may decree the compensation, to be paid as a lump sum or in instalments, according to the husband's ability to pay.

xiii. Yemen: Is a theocratic State, which declares Islam to be the official religion. Muslims of the Sunni sect constitute its majority. On the issue in hand, it has the following legislation in place:

Decree on Personal Status 1992

Decree 20 of 1992

Article 61. A divorce shall not be effective if pronounced by a man who is drunk, or has lost his senses, or has no power of discernment, if this is shown by his condition and action.

xxx xxx xxx

Article 64. A divorce to which a number is attached, whatever be the number, will effect only a single revocable divorce.

Article 65. The words saying that if the wife did or failed to do something she will stand divorced will not effect a divorce.

Article 66. The words that if an oath or vow is broken it will effect a divorce will not dissolve the marriage even if the said oath or vow is broken.

Article 67. A divorce can be revoked by the husband during the Iddat period. After the expiry of Iddat, a direct remarriage between them will be lawful.

xxx xxx xxx

Article 71. If a man arbitrarily divorces his wife without any reasonable ground and it causes hardship to her, the court may grant her compensation payable by the husband not exceeding maintenance for one year in accordance with her status. The court may decide if the compensation will be paid as a lump sum or in instalments.

B. Laws of Southeast Asian States

i. Indonesia: The Constitution of Indonesia guarantees freedom of religion among Indonesians. However, the Government recognizes only six official religions—Islam, Protestantism, Catholicism, Hinduism, Buddhism, and Confucianism. Muslims of the Sunni sect constitute its majority. On the issue in hand, it has the following legislation in place:

(a) Law of Marriage 1974

Law 1 of 1974

Article 38. A divorce shall be effected only in the court and the court shall not permit a divorce before attempting reconciliation between the parties. Divorce shall be permissible only for sufficient reasons indicating breakdown of marriage.

xxx xxx xxx

Article 41. In the event of a divorce both the parents shall continue to be responsible for the maintenance of their children. As regards custody of children, in case of a dispute between them the court shall take a decision. Expenses of maintenance and education shall be primarily the father's liability, but if he is unable to discharge this liability the court may transfer it to the mother. The court may also direct the former husband to pay alimony to the divorced wife.

(b) Marriage Regulations 1975

Regulation 9 of 1975

Article 14. A man married under Islamic law wanting to divorce his wife shall by a letter notify his intention to the District Court seeking proceedings for that purpose.

Article 15. On receiving a letter the court shall, within thirty days, summon the parties and gather from them all relevant facts.

Article 16. If the court is satisfied of the existence of any of the grounds mentioned in Article 19 below and is convinced that no reconciliation between the parties is possible it will allow a divorce.

Article 17. Immediately after allowing a divorce as laid down in Article 16 above the court shall issue a certificate of divorce and send it to the Registrar for registration of the divorce.

xxx xxx xxx

Article 19. A divorce may be allowed on the petition of either party if the other party:

(a) has committed adultery or become addict to alcohol, drugs, gambling or another serious vice;
(b) has deserted the aggrieved party for two years or more without any legal ground and against the said party's will;
(c) has been imprisoned for at least five years;
(d) has treated the aggrieved party with cruelty of an injurious nature;

(e) has been suffering from a physical deformity affecting conjugal duties, or where relations between the spouses have become too much strained making reconciliation impossible.

ii. Malaysia: Under the Constitution of Malaysia, Islam is the official religion of the country, but other religions are permitted to be practiced in peace and harmony. Muslims of the Sunni sect constitute its majority. On the issue in hand, it has the following legislation in place:

Islamic Family Law Act 1984

Act 304 of 1984

Article 47. (1) A husband or a wife who desires a divorce shall present an application for divorce to the court in the prescribed form accompanied by a statutory declaration containing (a) particulars of the marriage and the name, ages and sex of the children, if any, of the marriage; (b) particulars of the facts giving the court jurisdiction under Section 45; (c) particulars of any previous matrimonial proceedings between the parties, including the place of the proceedings; (d) a statement as to the reasons for desiring divorce; (e) a statement as to whether any, and if so, what steps have been taken to effect reconciliation; (f) the terms of any agreement regarding maintenance and habitation of the wife and the children of the marriage, if any, and the division of any assets acquired through the joint effort of the parties, if any, or where no such agreement has been reached, the applicant's proposals regarding those matters; and (g) particulars of the order sought.

(2) Upon receiving an application for divorce, the court shall cause summons to be served on the

other party together with a copy of the application and the statutory declaration made by the applicant, and the summons shall direct the other party to appear before the court so as to enable it to inquire whether or not the other party consents to the divorce.

(3) If the other party consents to the divorce and the court is satisfied after due inquiry and investigation that the marriage has irretrievably broken down, the court shall advise the husband to pronounce one Talaq before the court.

(4) The court shall record the fact of the pronouncement of one Talaq and shall send a certified copy of the record to the appropriate Registrar and to the Chief Registrar for registration.

(5) Where the other party does not consent to the divorce or it appears to the court that there is reasonable possibility of a reconciliation between the parties, the court shall as soon as possible appoint a Conciliatory Committee consisting of a religious officer as Chairman and two other persons, one to act for the husband and the other for the wife, and refer the case to the Committee.

(6) In appointing the two persons under sub-section (5) the court shall, where possible, give preference to close relatives of the parties having knowledge of the circumstances of the case.

(7) The court may give directions to the Conciliatory Committee as to the conduct of the conciliation and it shall conduct it in accordance with such directions.

(8) If the Committee is unable to agree or if the court is not satisfied with its conduct of the

conciliation, the court may remove the Committee and appoint another Committee in its place.

(9) The Committee shall endeavour to effect reconciliation within a period of six months from the date of its being constituted or such further period as may be allowed by the court.

(10) The Committee shall require the attendance of the parties and shall give each of them an opportunity of being heard and may hear such other persons and make such inquiries as it thinks fit and may, if it considers it necessary, adjourn its proceedings from time to time.

(11) If the Conciliatory Committee is unable to effect reconciliation and is unable to persuade the parties to resume their conjugal relationship, it shall issue a certificate to that effect and may append to the certificate such recommendations as it thinks fit regarding maintenance and custody of the minor children of the marriage, if any, regarding division of property and other matters related to the marriage.

(12) No advocate and solicitor shall appear or act for any party in any proceeding before a Conciliatory Committee and no party shall be represented by any person other than a member of his or her family without the leave of the Conciliatory Committee.

(13) Where the Committee reports to the court that reconciliation has been effected and the parties have resumed their conjugal relationship, the court shall dismiss the application for divorce.

(14) Where the Committee submits to the court a certificate that it is unable to effect reconciliation and to persuade the parties to resume the conjugal

relationship, the court shall advise the husband to pronounce one Talaq before the court, and where the court is unable to procure the presence of the husband before the court to pronounce one Talaq, or where the husband refuses to pronounce one Talaq, the court shall refer the case to the Hakams [arbitrators] for action according to section 48.

(15) The requirement of sub-section (5) as to reference to a Conciliatory Committee shall not apply in any case (a) where the applicant alleges that he or she has been deserted by an does not know the whereabouts of the other party; (b) where the other party is residing outside West Malaysia and it is unlikely that he or she will be within the jurisdiction of the court within six months after the date of the application; (c) where the other party is imprisoned for a term of three years or more; (d) where the applicant alleges that the other party is suffering from incurable mental illness; or (e) where the court is satisfied that there are exceptional circumstances which make reference to a Conciliatory Committee impracticable.

(16) Save as provided in sub-section (17), a Talaq pronounced by the husband or an order made by the court shall not be effective until the expiry of the Iddat.

(17) If the wife is pregnant at the time the Talaq is pronounced or the order is made, the Talaq or the order shall not be effective until the pregnancy ends.

iii. Philippines: Is a secular State. Christians constitute its majority. On the issue in hand, it has the following legislation in place:

Code of Muslim Personal Law 1977

Article 46. (1) A divorce by Talaq may be effected by the husband in a single repudiation of his wife during her Tuhr [non-menstrual period] within which he has totally abstained from carnal relations with her.

(2) Any number of repudiations made during one Tuhr [non-menstrual period] shall constitute only one repudiation and shall become irrevocable after the expiration of the prescribed Iddat.

(3) A husband who repudiates his wife, either for the first or second time, shall have the right to take her back within the Iddat period by resumption of cohabitation without need of a new contract of marriage. Should he fail to do so, the repudiation shall become irrevocable.

xxx xxx xxx

Article 85. Within seven days after the revocation of a divorce the husband shall, with the wife's consent, send a statement thereof to the Circuit Registrar in whose records the divorce was previously entered.

xxx xxx xxx

Article 161. (1) A Muslim male who has pronounced a Talaq shall, without delay, file with the Clerk of the Sharia Circuit Court of the place where his family resides a written notice of such fact and the circumstances attending thereto, after having served a copy to the wife concerned. The Talaq pronounced shall not become irrevocable until after the expiration of the prescribed Iddat.

(2) Within seven days from receipt of notice the Clerk of the Court shall require each of the parties

to nominate a representative. The representatives shall be appointed by the court to constitute, with the Clerk of the Court as Chairman, an Agama [religious scholars] Arbitration Council which shall try and submit to the court a report on the result of arbitration on the basis of which, and such other evidence as may be allowed, the court will pass an order.

(3) The provisions of this Article will be observed if the wife exercises right to Talaq-e-Tafweez.

xxx xxx xxx

Article 183. A person who fails to comply with the requirements of Article 85, 161 and 162 of this Code shall be penalized by imprisonment or a fine of two hundred to two thousand Pesos, or both.

C. Laws of Sub-continental States

i. Pakistan & Bangladesh: Are both theocratic States, wherein Islam is the official religion. In both countries Muslims of the Sunni sect constitute the majority. On the issue in hand, it has the following legislation in place:

Muslim Family Laws Ordinance 1961

Ordinance VIII of 1961 amended in Bangladesh by Ordinance 114 of 1985 (Bangladesh changes noted below relevant provisions)

Section 7. (1) Any man who wishes to divorce his wife shall, as soon as may be after the pronouncement of Talaq in any form whatsoever, give the Chairman a notice in writing of his having done so, and shall supply a copy thereof to the wife.

(2) Whoever contravenes the provision of sub-section (1) shall be punishable with simple imprisonment for a term which may extend to

one year, or with fine which may extend to five thousand rupees, or with both.

[Bangladesh: ten thousand taka]

(3) Save as provided in sub-section (5), a Talaq unless revoked earlier, expressly or otherwise, shall not be effective until the expiration of ninety days from the day on which notice under subsection (1) is delivered to the Chairman.

(4) Within thirty days of the receipt of notice under sub-section (1) the Chairman shall constitute an Arbitration Council for the purpose of bringing about reconciliation between the parties, and the Arbitration council shall take all steps necessary to bring about such reconciliation.

(5) If the wife be pregnant at the time Talaq is pronounced, Talaq shall not be effective until the period mentioned in sub-section (3) or of pregnancy, whichever is later, ends.

(6) Nothing shall debar a wife whose marriage has been terminated by Talaq effective under this section from re-marrying the same husband without any intervening marriage with a third person, unless such termination is for the third time so effective.

ii. Sri Lanka: Is a secular State. Buddhists constitute its majority. On the issue in hand, it has the following legislation in place:

Muslim Marriage and Divorce Act 1951 Act 6 of 1951 as amended by Act 40 of 2006

Section 17(4) Save as otherwise hereinafter expressly provided, every marriage contracted between Muslims after the commencement of this Act shall be registered, as hereinafter provided, immediately upon the conclusion of the Nikah ceremony connected therewith.

(5) In the case of each such marriage, the duty of causing it to be registered is hereby imposed upon the following persons concerned in the marriage; (a) the bridegroom, (b) the guardian of the bride, and (c) the person who conducted the Nikah ceremony connected with the marriage. Section 27. Where a husband desires to divorce his wife the procedure laid down in Schedule II shall be followed.

(2) Where a wife desires to effect a divorce from her husband on any ground not referred to in sub-section (1), being a divorce of any description permitted to a wife by the Muslim law governing the sect to which the parties belong, the procedure laid down in the Schedule III shall be followed so far as the nature of the divorce claimed in each case renders it possible or necessary to follow that procedure.

30. Rashid Ahmad v. Anisa Khatun: AIR 1932 PC 25

[...]

(iv) The conclusion: The Privy Council, upheld as valid, 'talaq-e-biddat' – triple talaq, pronounced by the husband, in the absence and without the knowledge of the wife, even though the husband and wife continued to cohabit for 15 long years thereafter, wherefrom 5 offsprings were born to them.

31. Jiauddin Ahmed v. Anwara Begum: (1981) 1 Gau L.R. 358 (Single Judge judgment, authored by Baharul Islam, J., as His Lordship then was).

[...]

A perusal of the conclusion recorded by the High Court, through the above observations, leaves no room for any doubt, that the 'talaq-e-biddat' pronounced by the husband without reasonable cause, and without being preceded by attempts of reconciliation, and without the involvement of arbitrators with due representation on behalf of the husband and wife, would not lead to a valid divorce.

32. Must. Rukia Khatun v. Abdul Khalique Laskar (1981) 1 Gau. L.R. 375, (Division Bench judgment, authored by Baharul Islam, CJ., as His Lordship then was).

[...]

(iv) The conclusion: [...] [T]he High Court recorded the following conclusion:

11. In our opinion the correct law of 'talaq' as ordained by Holy Quran is: (i) that 'talaq' must be for a reasonable cause; and (ii) that it must be preceded by an attempt at reconciliation between the husband and wife by two arbiters, one chosen by the wife from her family and the other by the husband from his. If their attempts fail, 'talaq' may be effected. In our opinion the Single Judge has correctly laid down the law in Criminal Revision No. 199/77 (supra), and, with respect the Calcutta High Court in ILR 59 Calcutta 833 and the Bombay High Court in ILR 30 Bombay 537 have not laid down the correct law.

33. Masroor Ahmed v. State (NCT of Delhi): 2008 (103) DRJ 137, (Single Bench judgment, authored by Badar Durrez Ahmed, J., as he then was).

[...]

A perusal of the conclusions recorded by the High Court would reveal, that triple talaq pronounced at the same time, is to be treated as a single pronouncement of divorce.

34. Nazeer v. Shemeema: 2017 (1) KLT 300, (Single Bench judgment, authored by A. Muhamed Mustaque, J.).

[...]

A perusal of the conclusions drawn by the High Court reveals, that the practice of 'talaq-e-biddat', was deprecated by the Court. The Court however called upon the legislature, to codify the law on the issue, as would result in the advancement of justice, as a matter of institutional form.

36. Mr. Amit Singh Chadha [...] [contended] that Articles 25, 26 and 29 of the Constitution, did not in any manner, impair the jurisdiction of this Court, to set right the apparent breach of constitutional morality. In this behalf, the Court's attention was invited to the fact, that Article 25 itself postulates, that the freedoms contemplated thereunder, were subject to the overriding principles enshrined in Part III – Fundamental Rights, of the Constitution.

39. Mr. Anand Grover, Senior Advocate, represented Zakia Soman – respondent no. 10. [...] [He] submitted, that the practice of 'talaq-e-biddat' was traceable to the second century, after the advent of Islam. It was asserted, that 'talaq-e-biddat' is recognized only by a few Sunni schools, including the Hanafi school. In this behalf, it was also brought to our notice, that most of the Muslims in India belonged to the Hanafi school of Sunni Muslims.

43. Based on the above submissions, it was contended [by Mr. Grover], that the judgment rendered by the Privy Council in the Rashid Ahmad case with reference to the validity of 'talaq-e-biddat' needed to be overruled. Since 'talaq-e-biddat' cannot be traced to the Quran, and since the Prophet himself deprecated it, and since 'talaq-e-biddat' was considered sinful by all schools of Sunni Muslims, and as invalid by all the Shia Muslim schools, it could not be treated to be a part of Muslim 'personal law'.

44. Ms. Indira Jaising, Senior Advocate, was the third counsel to represent the cause of the petitioners. She entered appearance on behalf of respondent no. 7 – Centre for Study of Society and Secularism[.]

45. It was submitted [by Ms. Jaising], that insofar as Muslim 'personal law' is concerned, it could no longer be treated as 'personal law', because it had been statutorily declared as "rule of decision" by Section 2 of the Shariat Act. It was therefore asserted, that all questions pertaining to Muslims, 'personal law' having been described as "rule of decision" could no longer be treated as private matters between parties, nor can they be treated as matters of mere 'personal law'.

50. Mr. Salman Khurshid, Senior Advocate, appearing as an intervener, submitted, that for searching a solution to a conflict, or for the resolution of a concern under Islamic law, reference had first to be made to the Quran. The availability of an answer to the disagreement, from the text of the Quran, has to be treated as a final pronouncement on the issue. When there is no clear guidance from the Quran, reference must be made to the traditions of the Prophet Muhammad – 'sunna', as recorded in the 'hadiths'. If no guidance is available on the issue, even from the 'hadiths', reference must then be made to the general consensus of opinion – 'ijma'. If a resolution to the dispute is found in 'ijma', it should be considered as a final view on the conflicting issue, under Islamic law. It was submitted, that the precaution that needed to be adopted while referring to 'hadiths' or 'ijma', was that neither of the two can derogate from the position depicted in the Quran.

51. [...] It was emphasised that the concept of 'talaq-e-biddat' (also described as irregular talaq), was based on the limit of three talaqs available to a man, namely, that a man can divorce the same wife (woman) three times in his life time. The first two are revocable within the period of 'iddat', whereas, the third talaq was irrevocable.

52. It was also submitted, that even if one examines the deeds of the Prophet Muhammad's companions, it was quite clear from the 'hadiths', that the same were followed during Caliph Abu

Bakr's time, and also during the first two years of Caliph Umar. But thereafter, only to meet an exigency, Caliph Umar started accepting the practice of pronouncing three divorces in one sitting, as final and irrevocable.

53. It was also the contention of learned senior Counsel, that [...] [t]he main idea in the procedure for divorce, as laid down by Islam, it was submitted, was to give the parties an opportunity for rapprochement. If three pronouncements are treated as a 'mughallazah' – divorce, then no opportunity is available to the spouses, to retrieve a decision taken in haste.

54. It was submitted, if the immediate concern about triple talaq could be addressed, by endorsing a more acceptable alternate interpretation, based on a pluralistic reading of the sources of Islam, i.e., by taking a holistic view of the Quran and the 'hadith' as indicated by various schools of thought (not just the Hanafi school), it would be sufficient for the purpose of ensuring justice to the petitioners, and others similarly positioned as them.

56. While advancing his aforesaid contention, there was also a note of caution expressed by learned senior counsel. It was pointed out, that it was not the role of a court, to interpret Muslim 'personal law' – Shariat. [...] It was submitted, that the role of a court, not being a body well versed in the intricacies of faith, would not extend to an interpretation of either the Quran or the 'hadiths', and therefore, 'talaq-e-biddat' should also be interpreted on the touchstone of reasonableness, in tune with the prevailing societal outlook.

65. [...] [T]he learned Attorney General placed reliance on Valsamma Paul v. Cochin University: (1996) 3 SCC 545 and drew the Court's attention to the following:

> 16. [...] To construe law one must enter into its spirit, its setting and history. Law should be capable to expand freedom of the people and the legal order can weigh with

utmost equal care to provide the underpinning of the highly inequitable social order. Judicial review must be exercised with insight into social values to supplement the changing social needs. The existing social inequalities or imbalances are required to be removed readjusting the social order through Rule of law ...

67. It was the emphatic assertion of the learned Attorney General, that freedom of religion was subservient to fundamental rights. It was contended in this behalf, that the words employed in Article 25(1) of the Constitution, which conferred the right to practice, preach and propagate religion were "subject to the provisions of this Part", which meant that the above rights are subject to Articles 14 and 15, which guarantee equality and non-discrimination.

69. It was emphasised by the learned Attorney General, that it was necessary to draw a line between religion per se, and religious practices. It was submitted, that the latter were not protected under Article 25.

[...]

In order to support the above view, the Court's attention was also drawn to the Javed case: (2003) 8 SCC 369, wherein this Court observed as under:

49. In State of Bombay v. Narasu Appa Mali [AIR 1952 Bom 84: 53 Cri LJ 354] the constitutional validity of the Bombay Prevention of Hindu Bigamous Marriages Act (25 of 1946) was challenged on the ground of violation of Articles 14, 15 and 25 of the Constitution. A Division Bench, consisting of Chief Justice Chagla and Justice Gajendragadkar (as His Lordship then was), held:

A sharp distinction must be drawn between religious faith and belief and religious practices. What the State protects is religious faith and belief. If religious practices run counter to

> public order, morality or health or a policy of social welfare upon which the State has embarked, then the religious practices must give way before the good of the people of the State as a whole.

70. [...] It was submitted, that the meaning of "law" as defined in clauses (2) and (3) of Article 13 is not exhaustive, and should be read as if it encompassed within its scope, 'personal law' as well.

71. It was acknowledged, that the legal position expressed in the Narasu Appa Mali case: AIR 1952 Bom 84 had been affirmed by this Court, on various occasions. Rather than recording the learned Attorney General's submissions in our words, we would extract the position acknowledged in the written submissions filed on behalf of the Union of India, in this matter, below:

> (e) Pertinently, despite this ruling that was later followed in Krishna Singh v. Mathura Ahir, (1981) 3 SCC 689 and Maharshi Avdhesh v. Union of India, (1994) Supp (1) SCC 713, the Supreme Court has actively tested personal laws on the touchstone of fundamental rights in cases such as Daniel Latifi v. Union of India, (2001) 7 SCC 740 (5-Judge Bench), Mohd. Ahmed Khan v. Shah Bano Begum, (1985) 2 SCC 556 (5-Judge Bench), John Vallamatom v. Union of India, (2003) 6 SCC 611 (3-Judge Bench) etc.[...]
>
> [...] It was also asserted, that this Court had further held, "Personal laws are derived not from the Constitution but from the religious scriptures. The laws thus derived must be consistent with the Constitution lest they become void under Article 13 if they violate fundamental rights."

72. [...] The test of what amounts to an essential religious practice, it was submitted, was laid down in a catena of judgments including Commissioner, Hindu Religious Endowments, Madras v. Sri Lakshmindra Thirtha Swamiar of Shirur Mutt: AIR 1954SC 282, wherein this Court held as under:

> 20. [...] In such cases, as Chief Justice Latham pointed out, the provision for protection of religion was not an absolute protection to be interpreted and applied independently of other provisions of the Constitution. These privileges must be reconciled with the right of the State to employ the sovereign power to ensure peace, security and orderly living without which constitutional guarantee of civil liberty would be a mockery.

[...]

Learned Attorney General also cited, State of Gujarat v. Mirzapur Moti Kureshi Kassab Jamat: (2005) 8 SCC 534, and placed reliance on the following observations:

> 22. In State of W.B. v. Ashutosh Lahiri [(1995) 1 SCC 189] this Court has noted that sacrifice of any animal by Muslims for the religious purpose on BakrI'd does not include slaughtering of cows as the only way of carrying out that sacrifice. Slaughtering of cows on BakrI'd is neither essential to nor necessarily required as part of the religious ceremony. An optional religious practice is not covered by Article 25(1).

77. It is also necessary for us to recount an interesting incident that occurred during the course of hearing. The learned Attorney General having assisted this Court in the manner recounted above, was emphatic that the other procedures available to Muslim men for obtaining divorce, such as, 'talaq-e-ahsan' and 'talaq-e-hasan' were also liable to be declared as unconstitutional, for the same reasons as have been expressed with reference to 'talaq-e-biddat'. In this behalf, the contention advanced was, that just as 'talaq-e-biddat', 'talaq-e-ahsan' and 'talaq-e-hasan' were based on the unilateral will of the husband, neither of these forms of divorce required the availability of a reasonable cause with the husband to divorce his wife, and neither of these needed the knowledge and/or notice of the wife, and in neither of these procedures

the knowledge and/or consent of the wife was required. And as such, the other two so-called approved procedures of divorce ('talaq-e-ahsan' and 'talaq-e-hasan') available to Muslim men, it was submitted, were equally arbitrary and unreasonable, as the practice of 'talaq-e-biddat'. [...] It was contended, that the challenge to 'talaq-e-ahsan' and 'talaq-e-hasan' would follow immediately after this Court had rendered its pronouncement with reference to 'talaq-e-biddat'. We have referred to the incident, and considered the necessity to record it, because of the response of the learned Attorney General to a query raised by the Bench. One of us (U.U. Lalit, J.), enquired from the learned Attorney General, that if all the three procedures referred to above, as were available to Muslim men to divorce their wives, were set aside as unconstitutional, Muslim men would be rendered remediless in matters of divorce? The learned Attorney General answered the query in the affirmative. But assured the Court, that the Parliament would enact a legislation within no time, laying down grounds on which Muslim men could divorce their wives. We have accordingly recorded the above episode, because it has relevance to the outcome of the present matter.

79. The submissions advanced on behalf of the Petitioners, were first of all sought to be repudiated by the AIMPLB – respondent no. 8 (hereinafter referred to as the AIMPLB). Mr. Kapil Sibal, Senior Advocate, and a number of other learned counsel represented the AIMPLB. [...] Insofar as the Muslim women are concerned, reference was made to 'burqa' or 'hijab' worn by women, whereby women veil themselves, from the gaze of strangers. All these observances, are matters of faith, of those professing the religion.

80. It was pointed out, that the personal affairs referred to in the foregoing paragraph, fall in the realm of 'personal law'.

[...]

[...] It was conceded, on behalf of the AIMPLB, that 'personal laws' were per se subservient to legislation, and as such, 'personal laws' were liable to be considered as mandatory, with reference to numerous aspects of an individual's life, only in the absence of legislation.

81. Even though it was acknowledged, that legislation on an issue would override 'personal law' on the matter, it was pointed out, that in the absence of legislation 'personal laws' in the Indian context, could not be assailed on the basis of their being in conflict with any of the provisions contained in Part III of the Constitution – the Fundamental Rights. [...] It was submitted, that to affect a change in 'personal law', it was imperative to embark on legislation, as provided for through entry 5 of the Concurrent List in the Seventh Schedule, which provides – "marriage and divorce; infants and minors; adoption; wills, intestacy and succession; joint family and partition; all matters in respect of which parties in judicial proceedings were immediately before the commencement of this Constitution subject to their personal law."

82. [...] [R]eference was also made to Section 112 of the Government of India Act, 1915, wherein a clear distinction was sought to be drawn between 'personal laws' and 'customs having force of law'. Section 112, aforementioned is extracted hereunder:

> 112. Law to be administered in cases of inheritance and succession. – The high courts at Calcutta, Madras and Bombay, in the exercise of their original jurisdiction in suits against inhabitants of Calcutta, Madras or Bombay, as the case may be, shall, in maters of inheritance and succession to lands, rents and goods, and in matters of contract and dealing between party and party, when both parties are subject to the same personal law or custom having the force of law, decide according to that personal law or custom, and when the parties are subject to different personal laws or

customs having the force of law, decide according to the law or custom to which the defendant is subject.

84. […] It was pointed out, that none of these procedural forms, finds a reference in the Quran. It was asserted, that none of these forms is depicted even in the 'hadith'. It was acknowledged, that 'hadiths' declared talaq by itself, as not a good practice, and yet – recognized the factum of talaq, and its legal sanctity.

88. Based on the factual position recorded in the previous three paragraphs, it was submitted, that this Court should not attempt to interpret the manner in which the believers of the faith had understood the process for pronouncement of talaq. It was pointed out, that matters of faith should best be left to be interpreted by the community itself, in the manner in which its members understand their own religion.

92. Based on the 'hadiths' depicted in the foregoing, and in the paragraphs preceding thereto, it was submitted, that for the Hanafi school of Sunni Muslims 'talaq-e-biddat' – triple talaq was a part and parcel of their 'personal law', namely, a part and parcel of their faith, which they had followed generation after generation, over centuries. That being the position, it was submitted, that 'talaq-e-biddat' should be treated as the constitutionally protected fundamental right of Muslims, which could not be interfered with on the touchstone of being violative of the fundamental rights, enshrined in the Constitution – or for that matter, constitutional morality propounded at the behest of the Petitioners.

93. […] It was submitted, that in all the countries in which the practice of 'talaq-e-biddat' has been annulled or was being read down, as a matter of interpretation, the legislatures of the respective countries have interfered to bring in the said reform.

94. […] Based on the Constituent Assembly debates with reference to draft Article 35, which was incorporated in the Constitution as Article 44 […], it was submitted, that as expressed in Article 25(2)

(b), so also the debates of Article 44, the intent of the Constituent Assembly was to protect 'personal laws' of different communities by elevating their stature to that of other fundamental rights, however with the rider, that the legislature was competent to amend the same.

96. [I]t was contended, that the main object of the legislation was not to express the details of the Muslim 'personal law' – 'Shariat'. The object was merely to do away with customs and usages as were in conflict with Muslim 'personal law' – 'Shariat'. [...] It was submitted, that the above enactment [i.e. The Muslim Personal Law (Shariat) Application Act, 1937 (The Shariat Act)] did not decide what was, or was not, Muslim 'personal law' – 'Shariat'. It would therefore be a misnomer to consider that the Muslim Personal Law (Shariat) Application Act, 1937, in any way, legislated on the above subject. It was pointed out, that Muslim 'personal law' – 'Shariat' comprised of the declarations contained in the Quran, or through 'hadiths', 'ijmas' and 'qiyas' [...] A belief, according to learned senior counsel, which is practiced for 1400 years, is a matter of faith, and is protected under Article 25 of the Constitution. Matters of belief and faith, it was submitted, have been accepted to constitute the fundamental rights of the followers of the concerned religion.

97. While concluding his submissions, learned senior counsel also affirmed, that he would file an affidavit on behalf of the AIMPLB. The aforesaid affidavit was duly filed[.]

116. In our considered view, the matter would most certainly also require a fresh look, because various High Courts, having examined the practice of divorce amongst Muslims, by way of 'talaq-e-biddat', have arrived at the conclusion, that the judgment in the Rashid Ahmad case: AIR 1932 PC 25 was rendered on an incorrect understanding, of the Muslim 'personal law' – 'Shariat'.

...

121. [...] A challenge to 'talaq-e-biddat' obviously cannot be raised on this ground [i.e. on the ground that this form of talaq

is not mentioned in the Holy Quran]. We are satisfied, that the different approved practices of talaq among Muslims, have their origin in 'hadiths' and other sources of Muslim jurisprudence. And therefore, merely because it is not expressly provided for or approved by the Quran, cannot be a valid justification for setting aside the practice.

122. The petitioners actually call for a simple and summary disposal of the controversy, by requiring us to hold, that whatever is irregular and sinful, cannot have the sanction of law.

123. [...](ii) 'Devadasi' translated literally means, a girl dedicated to the worship and service of a diety or temple. The surrender and service of the 'Devadasi', in terms of the practice, was for life. This practice had also been in vogue since time immemorial, even though originally 'Devadasis' had a high status in society, because the Rulers/Kings of the time, were patrons of temples. [...]

(iii) So far as 'polygamy' is concerned, we are of the view that polygamy is well understood, and needs no elaboration.

124. We are of the view, that the practices referred to by the petitioners, to support their claim, need a further examination, to understand how the practices were discontinued. [...]

> (i) Insofar as the practice of 'Sati' is concerned, its practice reached alarming proportion between 1815–1818, it is estimated that the incidence of 'Sati' doubled during this period. A campaign to abolish 'Sati' was initiated by Christian missionaries (-like, William Carey), and by Hindu Brahmins (-like, Ram Mohan Roy). [...]
>
> [...]
>
> (iii) The last of the sinful practices brought to our notice was 'polygamy'. Polygamy was permitted amongst Hindus. In 1860, the Indian Penal Code made 'polygamy' a criminal offence. The Hindu Mariage Act was passed in 1955.

126. [...] The manner in which one learned counsel expressed the proposition, during the course of hearing, was very interesting. We may therefore record the submission exactly in the manner it was projected. Learned counsel for evoking and arousing the Bench's conscience submitted, "if something is sinful or abhorrent in the eyes of God, can any law by man validate it".

...

132. Mr. Anand Grover, Senior Advocate, reiterated and reaffirmed the position expressed in the four judgments (two of the Gauhati High Court, one of the Delhi High Court, and the last one of the Kerala High Court) to emphasize his submissions, as a complete justification for accepting the claims of the petitioners. [...] Referring to the Principles of Mohomedan Law by Sir Dinshaw Fardunji Mulla (LexisNexis, Butterworths Wadhwa, Nagpur, 20th edition), it was asserted, that the 'hadiths' relied upon by the AIMPLB (to which a reference will be made separately), were far – far removed from the time of the Prophet Mohammad.

133. Learned senior counsel also asserted, that as a historical fact Shia Muslims believe, that during the Prophet's time, and that of the First Caliph – Abu Baqhr, and the Second Caliph – Umar, pronouncements of talaq by three consecutive utterances were treated as one. (Reference in this behalf was made to "Sahih Muslim" compiled by Al-Hafiz Zakiuddin Abdul-Azim Al-Mundhiri, and published by Darussalam).

137. [...] Mr. Salman Khurshid, learned Senior Advocate also cautioned this Court, that it was not its role to determine the true intricacies of faith.

139. Having given our thoughtful consideration on the entirety of the issue, we are persuaded to accept the counsel of Mr. Kapil Sibal and Mr. Salman Khurshid, Senior Advocates. It would be appropriate for us, to refrain from entertaining a determination on the issue in hand, irrespective of the opinion expressed

in the four judgments relied upon by learned counsel for the petitioners, and the Quranic verses and 'hadiths' relied upon by the rival parties. We truly do not find ourselves, upto the task. We have chosen this course, because we are satisfied, that the controversy can be finally adjudicated, even in the absence of an answer to the proposition posed in the instant part of the consideration.

143. [...] The debate and discussion amongst Islamic jurists in the relevant 'hadiths' reveal, that the practice of triple talaq was certainly, in vogue amongst Muslims, whether it was considered and treated as irregular or sinful, is quite another matter. [...] The only debate in these articles was about the consistence or otherwise, of the practice of 'talaq-e-biddat' – with Islamic values. Not that, the practice was not prevalent. The ongoing discussion and dialogue, clearly reveal, if nothing else, that the practice is still widely prevalent and in vogue.

144. The fact, that about 90% of the Sunnis in India, belong to the Hanafi school, and that, they have been adopting 'talaq-e-biddat' as a valid form of divorce, is also not a matter of dispute. [...] Those following this practice have concededly allowed their civil rights to be settled thereon. 'Talaq-e-biddat' is practiced in India by 90% of the Muslims (who belong to the Hanafi school).

157. [I]t is not possible for us to accept, the contention advanced on behalf of the petitioners, that the questions/subjects covered by the Muslim Personal Law (Shariat) Application Act, 1937 ceased to be 'personal law' and got transformed into 'statutory law'.

160. [...] [I]t was conceded on behalf of the learned Attorney General for India, that the judgment rendered by the Bombay High Court in the Narasu Appa Mali case: AIR 1952 Bom 84, has been upheld by the Court in the Shri Krishna Singh case: (1981) 3 SCC 689 and the Maharshi Avadhesh cases: (1994) Suppl. (1) SCC 713, wherein, this Court had tested the 'personal

laws' on the touchstone of fundamental rights in the cases of Mohd. Ahmed Khan v. Shah Bano Begum: (1985) 2 SCC 556, (by a 5-Judge Constitution Bench), Daniel Latifi v. Union of India: (2001) 7 SCC 740 by a 5-Judge Constitution Bench), and in the John Vallamattom case: (2003) 6 SCC 611, (by a 3-Judge Division Bench).

162. To be fair to the learned Attorney General, it is necessary to record, that he contested the determination recorded by the Bombay High Court in the Narasu Appa Mali case: AIR 1952 Bom 84, and the judgments rendered by this Court affirming the same, by assuming the stance that the position needed to be revisited[.]

165. [...] We have not accepted, that after the enactment of the Shariat Act, the questions/subjects covered by the said legislation ceased to be 'personal law', and got transformed into 'statutory law'. Since we have held that Muslim 'personal law' – 'Shariat' is not based on any State Legislative action, we have therefore held, that Muslim 'personal law' – 'Shariat', cannot be tested on the touchstone of being a State action. Muslim 'personal law' – 'Shariat', in our view, is a matter of 'personal law' of Muslims, to be traced from four sources, namely, the Quran, the 'hadith', the 'ijma' and the 'qiyas'. None of these can be attributed to any State action. We have also already concluded, that 'talaq-e-biddat' is a practice amongst Sunni Muslims of the Hanafi school. A practice which is a component of the 'faith' of those belonging to that school. 'Personal law', being a matter of religious faith, and not being State action, there is no question of its being violative of the provisions of the Constitution of India[.]

166. One of the issues canvassed on behalf of the petitioners, which was spearheaded by the learned Attorney General for India, was on the ground, that the constitutional validity of the practice of 'talaq-e-biddat' – triple talaq, was in breach of constitutional morality. [...] It was submitted, that Hindu,

Christian, Zoroastrian, Buddhist, Sikh, Jain women, were not subjected to ouster from their matrimonial relationship, without any reasonable cause, certainly not, at the whim of the husband; certainly not, without due consideration of the views expressed by the wife, who had the right to repel a husband's claim for divorce. It was asserted, that 'talaq-e-biddat', vests an unqualified right with the husband, to terminate the matrimonial alliance forthwith, without any reason or justification.

170. The debates in the Constituent Assembly with reference to Article 25, leave no room for any doubt, that the framers of the Constitution were firm in making 'personal law' a part of the fundamental rights. With the liberty to the State to provide for social reform.

172. There can be no doubt, that the 'personal law' has been elevated to the stature of a fundamental right in the Constitution. And as such, 'personal law' is enforceable as it is. [...] It is judicially unthinkable for a Court, to accept any prayer to declare as unconstitutional (-or unacceptable in law), for any reason or logic, what the Constitution declares as a fundamental right. Because, in accepting the prayer(s), this Court would be denying the rights expressly protected under Article 25.

189. [...] [W]e are satisfied, that international conventions and declarations are of utmost importance, and have to be taken into consideration while interpreting domestic laws. But, there is one important exception to the above rule, and that is, that international conventions as are not in conflict with domestic law, alone can be relied upon. We are of the firm opinion, that the disputation in hand falls in the above exception. Insofar as 'personal law' is concerned, the same has constitutional protection. Therefore if 'personal law' is in conflict with international conventions and declarations, 'personal law' will prevail. The contention advanced on behalf of the petitioners to hold the practice of 'talaq-e-biddat', on account it being in conflict

with conventions and declarations to which India is a signatory can therefore not be acceded to.

191. [...] The Union of India, has also participated in the debate. It has adopted an aggressive posture, seeking the invalidation of the practice by canvassing, that it violates the fundamental rights enshrined in Part III of the Constitution, and by further asserting, that it even violates constitutional morality. During the course of hearing, the issue was hotly canvassed in the media. Most of the views expressed in erudite articles on the subject, hugely affirmed that the practice was demeaning. Interestingly even during the course of hearing, learned counsel appearing for the rival parties, were in agreement, and described the practice of 'talaq-e-biddat' differently as, unpleasant, distasteful and unsavory. The position adopted by others was harsher, they considered it as disgusting, loathsome and obnoxious. Some even described it as being debased, abhorrent and wretched.

193. Religion is a matter of faith, and not of logic. It is not open to a court to accept an egalitarian approach, over a practice which constitutes an integral part of religion.

195. [...] We cannot nullify and declare as unacceptable in law, what the Constitution decrees us, not only to protect, but also to enforce. The authority to safeguard and compel compliance, is vested under a special jurisdiction in constitutional Courts (-under Article 32, with the Supreme Court; and under Article 226, with the High Courts). Accepting the Petitioners prayers, would be in clear transgression of the constitutional mandate contained in Article 25.

196. [...] We have to be guarded, lest we find our conscience traversing into every nook and corner of religious practices, and 'personal law'. Can a court, based on a righteous endeavour, declare that a matter of faith, be replaced – or be completely done away with. In the instant case, both prayers have been made.

197. We have arrived at the conclusion, that the legal challenge raised at the behest of the petitioners must fail, on the judicial front. Be that as it may, the question still remains, whether this is a fit case for us to exercise our jurisdiction under Article 142, "... for doing complete justice ...", in the matter.

199. In view of the position expressed above, we are satisfied, that this is a case which presents a situation where this Court should exercise its discretion to issue appropriate directions under Article 142 of the Constitution.

200. Till such time as legislation in the matter is considered, we are satisfied in injuncting Muslim husbands, from pronouncing 'talaq-e-biddat' as a means for severing their matrimonial relationship. The instant injunction, shall in the first instance, be operative for a period of six months.

* * *

Many people believe that legislation has been mandated by the Court. It was perhaps the sequence in which the judgments were pronounced, with the Chief Justice being the first to read the operative part of his judgment the word went out that Parliament was asked to legislate and that impression has stuck. The fact remains that along with Justice Kurian Joseph, the Chief Justice was in the majority of three against two in holding that Personal Law is a Fundamental Right.

* * *

Justice Kurian Joseph

202. What is bad in theology was once good in law but after Shariat has been declared as the personal law, whether what is Quranically wrong can be legally right is the issue to be considered in this case.

205. [...] The 1937 Act simply makes Shariat applicable as the rule of decision in the matters enumerated in section 2. Therefore, while talaq is governed by Shariat, the specific grounds and procedure for talaq have not been codified in the 1937 Act.

206. [...] I wholly agree with the learned Chief Justice that the 1937 Act is not a legislation regulating talaq. Consequently, I respectfully disagree with the stand taken by Nariman, J. that the 1937 Act is a legislation regulating triple talaq and hence, the same can be tested on the anvil of Article 14.

207. Shariat, having been declared to be Muslim Personal Law by the 1937 Act, we have to necessarily see what Shariat is. This has been beautifully explained by the renowned author, Asaf A.A. Fyzee in his book Outlines of Muhammadan Law, 5th Edition, 2008 at page 10.

> [...] We have the Qur'an which is the very word of God. Supplementary to it we have Hadith which are the Traditions of the Prophet—the records of his actions and his sayings—from which we must derive help and inspiration in arriving at legal decisions.

210. Sura LXV of the Quran deals with talaq. It reads as follows:

> [...]
> 2. Thus when they fulfill
> Their term appointed,
> Either take them back
> On equitable terms
> Or part with them
> On equitable terms;
> And take for witness
> Two persons from among you,
> Endued with justice
> And for those who fear
> God, He (ever) prepares
> A way out,
> [...]

6. Let the women live
(In 'iddat) in the same
Style as ye live,
According to your means:
Annoy them not, so as
To restrict them.
And if they carry (life
In their wombs), then
Spend (your substance) on them
Until they deliver
Their burden: and if
They suckle your (offspring),
Give them their recompense:
And take mutual counsel
Together, according to
What is just and reasonable.
And if ye find yourselves
In difficulties, let another
Woman suckle (the child)
On the (father's) behalf.

[...]

Sura II contains the following verses pertaining to divorce:

[...]

228. Divorced women
Shall wait concerning themselves
For three monthly periods.
Nor is it lawful for them
To hide what God
Hath created in their wombs,
If they have faith
In God and the Last Day.
And their husbands
Have the better right
To take them back

In that period, if
They wish for reconciliation.
And women shall have rights
Similar to the rights
Against them, according
To what is equitable;

[...]

229. A divorce is only
Permissible twice: after that,
The parties should either hold
Together on equitable terms,
Or separate with kindness.

[...]

231. When ye divorce
Women, and they fulfill
The term of their ('Iddat),
Either take them back
On equitable terms
Or set them free
On equitable terms;
But do not take them back
To injure them, (or) to take
Undue advantage;
If anyone does that,
He wrongs his own soul.
Do not treat God's Signs
As a jest,
But solemnly rehearse
God's favours on you,
And the fact that He
Sent down to you
The Book
And Wisdom,
For your instruction.

214. [...] No doubt, Sowaramma was not a case on triple talaq, however, the issue has been discussed in the judgment in paragraph 7 which has also been quoted in Shamim Ara.

> ... The view that the Muslim husband enjoys an arbitrary, unilateral power to inflict instant divorce does not accord with Islamic injunctions. ... It is a popular fallacy that a Muslim male enjoys, under the Quoranic law, unbridled authority to liquidate the marriage. 'The whole Quoran expressly forbids a man to seek pretexts for divorcing his wife, so long as she remains faithful and obedient to him, "if they (namely, women) obey you, then do not seek a way against them".' (Quoran IV: 34). The Islamic law gives to the man primarily the faculty of dissolving the marriage, if the wife, by her indocility or her bad character, renders the married life unhappy; but in the absence of serious reasons, no man can justify a divorce, either in the eye of religion or the law. If he abandons his wife or puts her away in simple caprice, he draws upon himself the divine anger, for the curse of God, said the Prophet, rests on him who repudiates his wife capriciously."

218. The High Court of Andhra Pradesh, in Zamrud Begum v. K. Md. Haneef and another: (2003) 3 ALD 220, is one of the first High Courts to affirm the view adopted in Shamim Ara. [...]

> 13. It is observed by the Supreme Court in the above said decision that talaq may be oral or in writing and it must be for a reasonable cause. It must be preceded by an attempt of reconciliation of husband and wife by two arbitrators one chosen from the family of the wife and other by husband. If their attempts fail then talaq may be effected by pronouncement.

224. Therefore, I find it extremely difficult to agree with the learned Chief Justice that the practice of triple talaq has to be considered integral to the religious denomination in question and that the same is part of their personal law.

225. [...] Except to the above extent, the freedom of religion under the Constitution of India is absolute and on this point, I am in full agreement with the learned Chief Justice. However, on the statement that triple talaq is an integral part of the religious practice, I respectfully disagree.

In any case, after the introduction of the 1937 Act, no practice against the tenets of Quran is permissible. Hence, there cannot be any Constitutional protection to such a practice and thus, my disagreement with the learned Chief Justice for the constitutional protection given to triple talaq.

226. [T]he process of harmonizing different interests is within the powers of the legislature. Of course, this power has to be exercised within the constitutional parameters without curbing the religious freedom guaranteed under the Constitution of India. However, it is not for the Courts to direct for any legislation.

* * *

Having concluded that triple talaq was no part of Shariah, Justice Joseph did not have to grapple with the 'bad in theology, good in law' argument. However, even if he had to pronounce on that, I imagine he would treat it differently from the traditional 'law and morality' debate that students of jurisprudence have continued to strive for an answer to, from the time of Lord Devlin[2].

* * *

Justice Rohinton Nariman (Justice U.U. Lalit Concurring)

230. [...] The neat question that arises before this Court is, therefore, whether the 1937 Act can be said to recognize and enforce Triple Talaq as a rule of law to be followed by the Courts in India and if not whether Narasu Appa (supra) which states

that personal laws are outside Article 13(1) of the Constitution is correct in law.

235. Marriage in Islam is a contract, and like other contracts, may under certain circumstances, be terminated. There is something astonishingly modern about this – no public declaration is a condition precedent to the validity of a Muslim marriage nor is any religious ceremony deemed absolutely essential, though they are usually carried out. [...] Prophet Mahomed had declared divorce to be the most disliked of lawful things in the sight of God. The reason for this is not far to seek. Divorce breaks the marital tie which is fundamental to family life in Islam. Not only does it disrupt the marital tie between man and woman, but it has severe psychological and other repercussions on the children from such marriage.

239. Section 2 of the 1937 Act states:

> 2. Application of Personal law to Muslims. – Notwithstanding any custom or usage to the contrary, in all questions (save questions relating to agricultural land) regarding intestate succession, special property of females, including personal properly inherited or obtained under contract or gift or any other provision of Personal Law, marriage, dissolution of marriage, including talaq, ila, zihar, lian, khula and mubaraat, maintenance, dower, guardianship, gifts, trusts and trust properties, and wakfs (other than charities and charitable institutions and charitable and religious endowments) the rule of decision in cases where the parties are Muslims shall be the Muslim Personal Law (Shariat).

241. It can be seen that the 1937 Act is a pre-constitutional legislative measure which would fall directly within Article 13(1) of the Constitution of India[.]

242. [L]earned counsel for the Muslim Personal Board as well as other counsel supporting their stand have argued that, read in

light of the Objects and Reasons, the 1937 Act was not meant to enforce Muslim personal law, which was enforceable by itself through the Courts in India. The 1937 Act was only meant, as the non-obstante clause in Section 2 indicates, to do away with custom or usage which is contrary to Muslim personal law.

245. It is, therefore, clear that all forms of Talaq recognized and enforced by Muslim personal law are recognized and enforced by the 1937 Act. This would necessarily include Triple Talaq when it comes to the Muslim personal law applicable to Sunnis in India.

247. At this stage, it is necessary to refer to the recognition of Triple Talaq as a legal form of divorce in India, as applicable to Sunni Muslims. In an early Bombay case, Sarabai v. Rabiabai,: (1906) ILR 30 Bom 537, Bachelor, J. referred to Triple Talaq and said that "it is good in law though bad in theology".

248. It is thus clear that it is this view of the law which the 1937 Act both recognizes and enforces so as to come within the purview of Article 13(1) of the Constitution.

251. "Religion" has been given the widest possible meaning by this Court in Commissioner, Hindu Religious Endowments, Madras v. Sri Lakshmindra Thirtha Swamiar of Sri Shirur Mutt,: 1954 SCR 1005 at 1023–1024. In this country, therefore, atheism would also form part of "religion". But one important caveat has been entered by this Court, namely, that only what is an essential religious practice is protected under Article 25. A few decisions have laid down what constitutes an essential religious practice.

[...]

[...] [I]n Commissioner of Police v. Acharya Jagdishwarananda Avadhuta, 2004 (12) SCC 770, it was stated as under:

> [...] Test to determine whether a part or practice is essential to a religion is to find out whether the nature of

the religion will be changed without that part or practice. If the taking away of that part or practice could result in a fundamental change in the character of that religion or in its belief, then such part could be treated as an essential or integral part.

252. Applying the aforesaid tests, it is clear that Triple Talaq is only a form of Talaq which is permissible in law, but at the same time, stated to be sinful by the very Hanafi school which tolerates it.

According to Javed (supra), therefore, this would not form part of any essential religious practice. Applying the test stated in Acharya Jagdishwarananda (supra), it is equally clear that the fundamental nature of the Islamic religion, as seen through an Indian Sunni Muslim's eyes, will not change without this practice. Indeed, Islam divides all human action into five kinds, as has been stated by Hidayatullah, J. in his introduction to Mulla (supra).

[...]

[...] We have already seen that though permissible in Hanafi jurisprudence, yet, that very jurisprudence castigates Triple Talaq as being sinful. It is clear, therefore, that Triple Talaq forms no part of Article 25(1). This being the case, the submission on behalf of the Muslim Personal Board that the ball must be bounced back to the legislature does not at all arise in that Article 25(2)(b) would only apply if a particular religious practice is first covered under Article 25(1) of the Constitution.

255. [...] In Obergefell v. Hodges, 135 S. Ct. 2584 at 2605, decided on June 26, 2015, the U.S. Supreme Court put it thus:

> [...] The idea of the Constitution "was to withdraw certain subjects from the vicissitudes of political controversy, to place them beyond the reach of majorities and officials and to establish them as legal principles to be applied by the courts."

266. In Maneka Gandhi v. Union of India, (1978) 1 SCC 248 [...], after stating that various fundamental rights must be read together and must overlap and fertilize each other, Bhagwati, J., further amplified this doctrine as follows (at pages 283–284):

The nature and requirement of the procedure Under Article 21

> [...] The principle of reasonableness, which legally as well as philosophically, is an essential element of equality or non-arbitrariness pervades Article 14 like a brooding omnipresence and the procedure contemplated by Article 21 must answer the test of reasonableness in order to be in conformity with Article 14.

267. This was further clarified in A.L. Kalra v. Project and Equipment Corpn., (1984) 3 SCC 316, following Royappa (supra) and holding that arbitrariness is a doctrine distinct from discrimination. It was held:

> [...] An action per se arbitrary itself denies equal of (sic) protection by law. The Constitution Bench pertinently observed in Ajay Hasia case [(1981) 1 SCC 722: 1981 SCC (L&S) 258: AIR 1981 SC 487: (1981) 2 SCR 79: (1981) 1 LLJ 103] and put the matter beyond controversy when it said "wherever therefore, there is arbitrariness in State action whether it be of the Legislature or of the executive or of an 'authority' Under Article 12, Article 14 immediately springs into action and strikes down such State action".

268. That the arbitrariness doctrine contained in Article 14 would apply to negate legislation, subordinate legislation and executive action is clear from a celebrated passage in the case of Ajay Hasia v. Khalid Mujib Sehravardi, (1981) 1 SCC 722 (at pages 740–741):

[...]

This vital and dynamic aspect which was till then lying latent and submerged in the few simple but pregnant words of Article 14 was explored and brought to light in Royappa case [(1975) 1 SCC 485: 1975 SCC (L&S) 99: (1975) 3 SCR 616] and it was reaffirmed and elaborated by this Court in Maneka Gandhi v. Union of India [(1978) 1 SCC 248] where this Court again speaking through one of us (Bhagwati, J.) observed: (SCC pp. 283–84, para 7):

> [...] Article 14 strikes at arbitrariness in State action and ensures fairness and equality of treatment. The principle of reasonableness, which legally as well as philosophically, is an essential element of equality or non-arbitrariness pervades Article 14 like a brooding omnipresence.

270. Close upon the heels of [K.R. Lakshmanan (Dr.) v. State of T.N: (1996) 2 SCC 226], a discordant note was struck in State of A.P. v. McDowell & Co., (1996) 3 SCC 709. Another three Judge Bench, in repelling an argument based on the arbitrariness facet of Article 14, held:

> [...] The applicability of doctrine of proportionality even in administrative law sphere is yet a debatable issue. (See the opinions of Lords Lowry and Ackner in R. v. Secy. of State for Home Deptt., ex p Brind [1991 AC 696: (1991) 1 All ER 720] AC at 766–67 and 762.) It would be rather odd if an enactment were to be struck down by applying the said principle when its applicability even in administrative law sphere is not fully and finally settled. It is one thing to say that a restriction imposed upon a fundamental right can be struck down if it is disproportionate, excessive or unreasonable and quite another thing to say that the court can strike down enactment if it thinks it unreasonable, unnecessary or unwarranted. (at pages 737–739)

271. This judgment failed to notice at least two binding precedents, first, the judgment of a Constitution Bench in Ajay Hasia (supra) and second, the judgment of a coordinate three judge bench in Lakshmanan (supra). Apart from this, the reasoning contained as to why arbitrariness cannot be used to strike down legislation

as opposed to both executive action and subordinate legislation was as follows:

(1) According to the Bench in McDowell (supra), substantive due process is not something accepted by either the American courts or our courts and, therefore, this being a reiteration of substantive due process being read into Article 14 cannot be applied. A Constitution Bench in Mohd. Arif v. Supreme Court of India, (2014) 9 SCC 737, has held, following the celebrated Maneka Gandhi (supra), as follows:

> 27. The stage was now set for the judgment in Maneka Gandhi [Maneka Gandhi v. Union of India, [(1978) 2 SCR 621: (1978) 1 SCC 248]. Several judgments were delivered, and the upshot of all of them was that Article 21 was to be read along with other fundamental rights, and so read not only has the procedure established by law to be just, fair and reasonable, but also the law itself has to be reasonable as Articles 14 and 19 have now to be read into Article 21.
>
> 28. Close on the heels of Maneka Gandhi case [...] came Mithu v. State of Punjab [(1983) 2 SCC 277: 1983 SCC (Cri) 405], in which case the Court noted as follows: (SCC pp. 283–84, para 6)
>
> > '6. ... In Sunil Batra v. Delhi Admn. [(1978) 4 SCC 494: 1979 SCC (Cri) 155], while dealing with the question as to whether a person awaiting death sentence can be kept in solitary confinement, Krishna Iyer J. said that though our Constitution did not have a "due process" clause as in the American Constitution; the same consequence ensued after the decisions in Bank Nationalisation case'.

Clearly, therefore, the three Judge Bench has not noticed Maneka Gandhi (supra) cited in Mohd. Arif (supra) to show that the wheel has turned full circle and substantive due process is part of Article 21 as it is to be read with Articles 14 and 19.

Mathew, J., while delivering the first Tej Bahadur Sapru Memorial Lecture entitled "Democracy and Judicial Review", has pointed out:

> [...] I have had occasion to consider this question in Kesavananda Bharati's case. I said:
> When a court adjudges that a legislation is bad on the ground that it is an unreasonable restriction, it is drawing the elusive ingredients for its conclusion from several sources ... If you examine the cases relating to the imposition of reasonable restrictions by a law, it will be found that all of them adopt a standard which the American Supreme Court has adopted in adjudging reasonableness of a legislation under the due process clause.

In a long and illuminating concurring judgment, Krishna Iyer, J., added (at page 518):

> 52. True, our Constitution has no 'due process' clause or the VIII Amendment; but, in this branch of law, after R.C. Cooper v. Union of India, (1970) 1 SCC 248 and Maneka Gandhi v. Union of India, (1978) 1 SCC 248, the consequence is the same. For what is punitively outrageous, scandalizingly unusual or cruel and rehabilitatively counter-productive, is unarguably unreasonable and arbitrary and is shot down by Articles 14 and 19 and if inflicted with procedural unfairness, falls foul of Article 21.

A binding judgment of five learned Judges of this Court cannot be said to be of "no assistance" by stating that the decision turned mainly on Article 21, though Article 14 was also referred to. It is clear that the ratio of the said Constitution Bench was based both on Article 14 and

> Article 21 as is clear from the judgment of the four learned Judges in paragraphs 19 and 23 set out supra. A three Judge Bench in the teeth of this ratio cannot, therefore, be said to be good law.

[...] We have seen how this view was upset by an eleven Judge Bench of this Court in Rustom Cavasjee Cooper v. Union of India, (1970) 1 SCC 248, and followed in Maneka Gandhi (supra). Arbitrariness in legislation is very much a facet of unreasonableness in Article 19(2) to (6), as has been laid down in several Judgments of this Court, some of which are referred to in Om Kumar (infra) and, therefore, there is no reason why arbitrariness cannot be used in the aforesaid sense to strike down legislation under Article 14 as well.

[...]

[...] One more reason given is that the proportionality doctrine, doubtful of application even in administrative law, should not, therefore, apply to this facet of Article 14 in constitutional law. Proportionality as a constitutional doctrine has been highlighted in Om Kumar v. Union of India, (2001) 2 SCC 386 at 400–401 as follows:

> [...] "Reasonable restrictions" Under Articles 19(2) to (6) could be imposed on these freedoms only by legislation and courts had occasion throughout to consider the proportionality of the restrictions. In numerous judgments of this Court, the extent to which "reasonable restrictions" could be imposed was considered. [...] [T]he underlying purpose of the restrictions imposed, the extent and urgency of the evil sought to be remedied thereby, the disproportion of the imposition, the prevailing conditions at the time". This principle of proportionality vis-à-vis legislation was referred to by Jeevan Reddy, J. in State of A.P. v. McDowell & Co.
>
> [...]

> [...] This is again nothing but the principle of proportionality. There are also cases where legislation or rules have been struck down as being arbitrary in the sense of being unreasonable [see Air India v. Nergesh Meerza [(1981) 4 SCC 335: 1981 SCC (L&S) 599] (SCC at pp. 372–373)]. But this latter aspect of striking down legislation only on the basis of "arbitrariness" has been doubted in State of A.P. v. McDowell and Co.

272. The thread of reasonableness runs through the entire fundamental rights Chapter. What is manifestly arbitrary is obviously unreasonable and being contrary to the rule of law, would violate Article 14.

274. [...] [In Mardia Chemicals Ltd. & Ors. v. Union of India & Ors. etc. etc., (2004) 4 SCC 311 at 354, this Court struck down Section 17(2) of the Securitisation and Reconstruction of Financial Assets and Enforcement of Security Interest Act, 2002, as follows:

> [...] Such conditions are not only onerous and oppressive but also unreasonable and arbitrary. Therefore, in our view, sub-section (2) of Section 17 of the Act is unreasonable, arbitrary and violative of Article 14 of the Constitution.

276. In a Constitution Bench decision in Ashoka Kumar Thakur v. Union of India [(2008) 6 SCC 1 at 524], an extravagant argument that the impugned legislation was intended to please a Section of the community as part of the vote catching mechanism was held to not be a legally acceptable plea and rejected by holding that:

The validity of a constitutional amendment and the validity of plenary legislation have to be decided purely as questions of constitutional law. This Court in State of Rajasthan v. Union of India [: (1977) 3 SCC 592] said: (SCC p. 660, para 149)

> 149. ... if a question brought before the court is purely a political question not involving determination of any legal or constitutional right or obligation, the court would not entertain it, since the court is concerned only with adjudication of legal rights and liabilities.

277. While examining the validity of a legislation which deprives a person of property Under Article 300-A, this Court when faced with Mcdowell (supra) pointed out that (at page 58):

203. Even in *McDowell* case [(1996) 3 SCC 709], it was pointed out that some or other constitutional infirmity may be sufficient to invalidate the statute. A three-Judge Bench of this Court in *McDowell & Co.* case [(1996) 3 SCC 709] held as follows: (SCC pp. 737–38, para 43)

> [...] There is no third ground.... No enactment can be struck down by just saying that it is arbitrary or unreasonable. Some or other constitutional infirmity has to be found before invalidating an Act.

[...]

205. Plea of unreasonableness, arbitrariness, proportionality, etc. always raises an element of subjectivity on which a court cannot strike down a statute or a statutory provision, especially when the right to property is no more a fundamental right. Otherwise the court will be substituting its wisdom to that of the legislature, which is impermissible in our constitutional democracy.

278. In a recent Constitution Bench decision in Natural Resources Allocation, In re, Special Reference No. 1 of 2012, (2012) 10 SCC 1, this Court [...] went on to state that "arbitrariness" and "unreasonableness" have been used interchangeably as follows:

103. As is evident from the above, the expressions "arbitrariness" and "unreasonableness" have been used interchangeably and in fact, one has been defined in terms of the other. More recently, in Sharma Transport v. Govt. of A.P. [(2002) 2 SCC 188], this Court has observed thus: (SCC pp. 203–04, para 25)

> 25. ... In order to be described as arbitrary, it must be shown that it was not reasonable and manifestly arbitrary. The

expression 'arbitrarily' means: in an unreasonable manner, as fixed or done capriciously or at pleasure, without adequate determining principle, not founded in the nature of things, non-rational, not done or acting according to reason or judgment, depending on the will alone.
(at page 81)

After stating all this, it then went on to comment, referring to McDowell (supra) that no arbitrary use should be made of the arbitrariness doctrine. It then concluded (at page 83):

> [...] [A] State action has to be tested for constitutional infirmities qua Article 14 of the Constitution. The action has to be fair, reasonable, non-discriminatory, transparent, non-capricious, unbiased, without favouritism or nepotism, in pursuit of promotion of healthy competition and equitable treatment. It should conform to the norms which are rational, informed with reasons and guided by public interest, etc.

280. As has been noted by us earlier in this judgment, Mcdowell (supra) itself is per incuriam, not having noticed several judgments of Benches of equal or higher strength, its reasoning even otherwise being flawed. The judgments, following McDowell (supra) are, therefore, no longer good law.

281. To complete the picture, it is important to note that subordinate legislation can be struck down on the ground that it is arbitrary and, therefore, violative of Article 14 of the Constitution. In Cellular Operators Association of India v. Telecom Regulatory Authority of India, (2016) 7 SCC 703, this Court referred to earlier precedents, and held:

[...]

[...] [I]n Sharma Transport v. State of A.P. [(2002) 2 SCC 188], this Court held: (SCC pp. 203–04, para 25)

> 25. ... The tests of arbitrary action applicable to executive action do not necessarily apply to delegated legislation. In order to strike down a delegated legislation as arbitrary it has to be established that there is manifest arbitrariness.

282. [...] Manifest arbitrariness, therefore, must be something done by the legislature capriciously, irrationally and/or without adequate determining principle. Also, when something is done which is excessive and disproportionate, such legislation would be manifestly arbitrary. We are, therefore, of the view that arbitrariness in the sense of manifest arbitrariness as pointed out by us above would apply to negate legislation as well under Article 14.

283. Applying the test of manifest arbitrariness to the case at hand, it is clear that Triple Talaq is a form of Talaq which is itself considered to be something innovative, namely, that it is not in the Sunna, being an irregular or heretical form of Talaq.

284. Given the fact that Triple Talaq is instant and irrevocable, it is obvious that any attempt at reconciliation between the husband and wife by two arbiters from their families, which is essential to save the marital tie, cannot ever take place. [...] This form of Talaq must, therefore, be held to be violative of the fundamental right contained under Article 14 of the Constitution of India. In our opinion, therefore, the 1937 Act, insofar as it seeks to recognize and enforce Triple Talaq, is within the meaning of the expression "laws in force" in Article 13(1) and must be struck down as being void to the extent that it recognizes and enforces Triple Talaq. Since we have declared Section 2 of the 1937 Act to be void to the extent indicated above on the narrower ground of it being manifestly arbitrary, we do not find the need to go into the ground of discrimination in these cases, as was argued by the learned Attorney General and those supporting him.

* * *

Epilogue

I am certain that this case will not draw the blinds on the issue of religious rights, particularly of the country's minority religious populations. But it is at least able to contribute to a better understanding of the issue across social boundaries. What's more, it will give perspective on the debate and endeavours for the reform of institutions. In the life of a nation, there are some constants and many malleable dimensions. We are yet a young nation in the modern world, although we are an ancient civilization. For some people, the evolution of our nation's identity might have ended on a particular date in history, just as some Muslims believed that *ijtehad* came to an end several centuries ago. Neither view is, of course, true. Debate and reform must continue to recharge lend vitality to our composite heritage. India's strength will ultimately come not from its military prowess and economic dynamics, but its innate spiritual and philosophical dimensions. When the history of Indian law, or indeed the growth of our nation, is written about there will hopefully be a mention of the *Shayara Bano* case before the Constitutional Bench presided by Chief Justice J.S. Khehar. However, future generations of Supreme Court judges will need to tackle not only further conflicts between Personal Law and general provisions of law about equality, but also, more importantly, reflect on the role of faith versus faith.

Annexure

Nikah Nama[I]

A Nikah Nama (marriage contract) is a legal document certifying the solemnization of marriage between a man and woman with stipulations duly endorsed by Islamic Law.

Under the Enacted Muslim Family Law Act 2017, it is mandatory that the Nikah Nama is Registered with the local Union Authority recognized by The State and Central Government of India, where an original copy of Nikah Nama is kept as public record. In case Nikah Nama is lost a duplicate copy a certified and attested copy of it can obtained from the relevant Union Council where it was registered.

The Prescribed Nikah Nama will be Applicable throughout all Talukas, Districts, STATES THROUGHOUT INDIA. It can be translated into Urdu (or other languages) by Government appointed translators.

NIKAH NAMA OR DEED OF MARRIAGE CONTRACT 2017

NIKAH NAMA OR DEED OF MARRIAGE CONTRACT

1. Name of bridegroom (with latest photograph)
2. Full residential address of Bridegroom a copy of Aadhaar card or passport
3. How many years the Bridegroom has spent at the present address
4. Present Income of Bridegroom
5. Age of Bridegroom
6. Whether Bridegroom is a Widower, Divorcee
7. Business of Bridegroom if any with address or Name and address of Company or Employer
8. Approximate income of Bridegroom
9. Name of Bridegroom's father with Residence with photograph
10. Name of Bride with latest photograph, copy of Aadhaar card or passport
11. Present Address of Bride/Residence of Bride
12. Name of Bride's father with Residence with photograph
13. Age of Bride
14. Whether Bride is a Maiden, Widow or a Divorcee
15. Whether wife employed or self-employed
16. Name of Vakil appointed by Bride and his Present Address and photograph
17. Name of Vakil's father with photograph and his Residence

18. Name of Vakil appointed by the Bridegroom and his Present Address with photograph
19. Name of Vakil's father and his Residence with photograph
20. Name of Witnesses with photographs and addresses to the appointment of the Bride's and Bridegroom's Vakil, their Residences, their father's Residences and their relationship to the Bride and Bridegroom respectively
21. Name of Witnesses with (photographs) to the marriage, their father's names and both residences
22. Date, month and year on which marriage is contracted
23. Amount of Maher (should generally be fixed as Maher-i-Sunnah, unless otherwise agreed to between the parties)
24. How much of the Maher is Mu'ajjal or prompt and how much is Mu'wajjal or deferred
25. If Mu'ajjal or prompt, how much is paid at the time of marriage
26. Whether any property was paid in lieu of the whole or any portion of the Maher, with specification to the same and its valuation agreed to between the parties
27. Consent of Parties must be duly noted and signed
28. Special Conditions
    1. The girl must have reached of majority (18 years of age).
    2. A triple talak pronounced in one sitting is judicially null and void. A husband who pronounces such a talak is liable to pay a fine of Rs 50,000 and serve an imprisonment term up to 5 years.
    3. A marriage can be only be dissolved by a Judicial decree. Proceedings of a divorce can be initiated by either the husband or the wife.

4. In the case of intent an intent to divorce, the appointment of Arbitrators representing both parties to effect reconciliation is mandatory. The iddat or waiting period of 3 months is mandatory for the process of reconciliation. A divorce can be effected only by the judge/Kazi appointed and authorized by the Government of India only after the mandatory period of iddat. The iddat period cannot exceed 3 months.
5. A second marriage by the husband during the subsistence or continuance of the first marriage is illegal. Such a marriage will be declared null and void. On this ground, the wife can exercise her power of Talak-i-Tafwiz or Delegated Power to Divorce by the wife, to divorce the husband. This act by the husband shall be punishable by imprisonment extending to a period of 5 years or a fine of Rs 50,000 or both.
6. It is mandatory to incorporate a judicially enforceable stipulation of Talak-i-Tafwiz or Delegated Power to Divorce by the wife in the body of the Nikah Nama whereby the wife can claim Divorce or she can appoint a Vakil to effect a Divorce on her behalf. The Talak-i-Tafwiz will be unconditional.
7. The wife can employ herself in any respectable profession after marriage.
8. The wife can visit her parents, relatives on a regular basis.
9. Gifts in the form of cash, ornaments, clothes, or other articles given by the girl's parents, relations and friends to the girl as a gift on marriage shall be absolute property of the girl.

10. Ornaments, clothes, other articles, or cash given by the boy and his parents, relations to the girl as a gift on marriage unless otherwise specified in the contract shall be the absolute property of the girl.
11. Mata or a provision for maintenance should be provided for on a reasonable for the wife scale OR, a substantial amount can be awarded. In case of children, the father will be held responsible for their maintenance, whether or not the children live with him.
12. The mother will be the custodian of children, whether male or female unless she for specific reasons gives up this right.
13. Name and address of the State-appointed judge by whom the marriage was solemnized.
14. Address of office or jamat where marriage was solemnized.
15. Date of Registration of Marriage
16. Signature of Bridegroom
17. Signature of Bridegroom's Vakil

[...]

29. Signature of Bride
30. Signature of Bride's Vakil
31. Signature of Witnesses to marriage
32. Signature of the Judicial Appointee who solemnized marriage
33. Signature and Seal of Nikah Registrar
34. Talak-i-Tafwiz or Delegated Power to Divorce: I have appointed my wife _______________ daughter of __________________ as Vakil that she herself may for reasons mentioned below can claim Divorce or

she can appoint a Vakil to effect a Divorce on her behalf. Talak-i-Tafwiz or Delegated Power to Divorce: I have appointed my wife _____________ daughter of _________________ as Vakil that she herself may for reasons mentioned below can claim Divorce or she can appoint a Vakil to effect a Divorce on her behalf.

35. The proceedings of a divorce can be initiated by either the husband or the wife. The marriage will be dissolved only though the decree of a Judge.
36. Documentation of the above drawn up at the time of marriage relating to dower maintenance, etc, if so, contents thereof in brief.
37. The marriage will be registered by the registrar appointed by Government of India.

*Documentation of the above drawn up at the time of marriage relating to dower.
**Photographs and full addresses of Bride, Bridegroom, Vakil, Witnesses, Nikah official need to be attached to The Nikah Nama.

Brought forth through a comparative study of the various Nikah-Namas formulated by different sections of Muslims in India.
This Nikah-Nama [has been] compiled by Dr Zeenat Shaukat Ali,
Director General, The Wisdom Foundation
5th June 2017

Notes and References

Preface

1. T. Andhyarujina, *The Kesavananda Bharati Case: The Untold Story of Struggle for Supremacy by Supreme Court and Parliament* (New Delhi: Universal Law Publishing, 2011).
2. The European Court of Justice, while deciding two cases from Belgium, recently held that a workplace may ban wearing any political, philosophical, or religious sign as a matter of its general policy. *Belcacemi and Oussar v. Belgium*—ban on wearing face covering in public areas (Law of 1 June 2011) and *Dakir v. Belgium*—ban on wearing face veils in the public areas of three municipalities, both decided on 11 July 2017. The European Court of Human Rights (ECtHR), on the other hand, has previously held that wearing religious symbols is sometimes an employee's right to manifest freedom of religion.

3. Ronald Dworkin, *Religion without God* (Cambridge: Harvard University Press, 2013).
4. *Gilette v. United States*, 401 US 437 (1971).
5. *Torcaso v. Watkins*, 367 U.S. 488 (1961).
6. *Campbell and Cosans v. The United Kingdom*, Application No. 7511/76; 7743/76, decided on 25 February 1982, para 36.
7. Pacifism, veganism, and atheism were argued to be beliefs to be protected under the right to freedom of religion clause as early as 1978 in *Arrowsmith v. The United Kingdom*, No. 7050/75, decided on 12 October 1978; *W. v. The United Kingdom*, No. 18187/91, decided on 10 February 1993; and *Angeleni v. Sweden*, No. 10491/83, decided on 3 December 1986.
8. *Kokkinakis v. Greece*, App. location No. 14307/88, decided on 25 May 1993, Para 31.
9. Dworkin, '*Religion without God*'.
10. *The Commissioner, Hindu Religious Endowments, Madras v. Sri Lakshmindra Thirtha Swamiar of Sri Shirur Mutt* (1954) SCR 1005.
11. See Justice Jagdish Singh Khehar opinion in the minority judgment in *Shayara Bano v. Union of India* Writ Petition (C) No. 118 of 2016.
12. (1996) 9 SCC 548.
13. (1996) 9 SCC 549, [86].
14. (2004) 12 SCC 770.

Introduction

1. Writ Petition (C) No. 118 of 2016.
2. *Masroor Ahmad v. State (NCT of Delhi) and Another* 2008 (103) DRJ 137.
3. *Mohammed Zubai Corporal No. 781467-G v Union of India* Civil Appeal No. 8644 of 2009.

4. The 'rule of three' in the context of literature refers to the principle that suggests how events or characters, when introduced in threes, are more effective in the execution of the story. They are considered to be more humorous, more satisfying, and to have a greater impact on the reader in terms of how well they engage.

Chapter I: He Said, She Said, They Said: Arguments before the Court

1. (1985) 2 SCC 556.
2. *Ranjit D. Udeshi v State of Maharashtra* AIR 1965 SC 881.
3. The movement begun by Maulana Nadvi to 'disseminate the message of love and amity among the people of India' (http://www.milligazette.com/Archives/15-1-2000/Art17.htm).
4. AIR 1954 SC282.
5. AIR 1972 All 273.
6. (1996) 5 SCC 25.
7. (1997) 3 SCC 573.
8. 1994 Supp (1) SCC 713.
9. 1951 SCC OnLine Bom72.
10. While the Babri Masjid–Ram Janmabhoomi dispute spans multiple decades and cases, here I refer to the Board's handling of the matter post the decisions of the Allahabad High Court on 30 September 2010.
11. *Acharya Jagdishwaran and Avadhuta and Others v. Commissioner of Police, Calcutta and Another* (1983) 4 SCC 522.
12. *Bijoe Emmanuel and Others v. State of Kerela and Others* (1986) 3 SCC 615.
13. The Moral Reading of the Constitution, *New York Review of Books*, 21 March 1966.
14. *Brown v. Board of Education of Topeka*, 347 US 483.

15. See, for example, Richard E. Posner 'The Incoherence of Antonin Scalia', *New Republic*, 24 August 2012 (https://newrepublic.com/article/106441/scalia-garner-reading-the-law-textual-originalism); or Jebediah Purdy 'Scalia's Contradictory Originalism', *The New Yorker*, 16 February 2016 (https://www.newyorker.com/news/news-desk/scalias-contradictory-originalism).
16. AIR 1954 SC 282.
17. (2004) 12 SCC 770.
18. *Masroor Ahmad v. State (NCT of Delhi) and Another* 2008 (103) DRJ 137.
19. Shweta Bansal, *'Courting Politics'* (Eastern Book Company, 2017).

Chapter 2: Triple Talaq: Bad in Theology, Good in Law

1. See Ronald Dworkin, *'Religion without God'* (Cambridge: Harvard University Press, 2013).
2. *Dr Ramesh Yeshwant Prabhoo v. Prabhakar Kashinath Kunte and Others* (1996) 1 SCC 390.
3. *Abhiram Singh v. CD Commachen* (2017) 2 SCC 629.
4. http://www.dictionary.com/browse/religion.
5. https://www.merriam-webster.com/dictionary/religion.
6. Clifford Geertz, *An Interpretation of Cultures* (Perseus Books Group, 2000).
7. Syed Amir Ali, *Mahommedan Law*, 5th Edition (Kitab Bhavan).
8. The largest of the Shia factions, to whom a majority of Shias belong, who believe that twelfth Imam entered a state of occultation, or hiddenness, in 939 and that he will return at the end of time.
9. Ameer Ali, *Muhammadan Law, Vol. 2* (Kitab Bhawan, 1986)

10. Dr Zeenat Shaukat Ali, *Marriage and Divorce in Islam* (Mumbai: Jaico Publications, 1987); see Annexure 2.
11. Imam Muslim Ibn Al-Hajjaj, *Sahih Muslim* (Darussalam, 2007); translated by Nasiruddin Al-Khattab.
12. 2010 SCC OnLine Gau 147.
13. 2003 (1) BomCR 740.
14. AIR 1971 Ker 261.
15. Radd-ul-Muhtar as quoted in Syed Ameer Ali, *Muhammadan Law, Vol. 2* (New Delhi: Kitab Bhawan, 1986), p. 241.
16. Sura No. 96 (Verses 1–5).
17. The ninth day of the twelfth and final month of the Islamic calendar in the year ten (corresponding to the year 632 CE).
18. See Sayyid Ali Ashgar Razwy, *A Restatement of the History of Islam and Muslims* (Lulu Press, 2014).
19. Shah Wali-Allah, *Fuyud al-Haramain* (as quoted by Dr Riaz-ul-Hasan Gilani in *The Reconstruction of Legal Thought in Islam* (Markazi Maktaba Islami Publishers, 2006).
20. *Masrat Begum v. Abdul Rashid Khan & Anr*. 561-A Cr. PC no.110 of 2010 & Cr. MP no. 239 of 2010, High Court of Jammu and Kashmir at Srinagar.
21. *Sahih Muslim*.
22. *Sahih Muslim*.
23. Aqil Ahmad, *Text Book on Mohammedan Law* (Central Law Agency, 2006).
24. Hafiz Ibn Kathir, *Tafsir Ibn Kathir*, (Darussalam, 2003); translated under the supervision of Sheikh Safiur-Rahman Al-Mubarakpuri.
25. Kathir, *Tafsir Ibn Kathir* (2003).
26. Quoted from the judgment of Justice Baharul Islam, in *Sri. Jiauddin Ahmed v. Mrs. Anwara Begum*, (1981) 1 GLR 358.
27. Quoted from the judgment of Justice Baharul Islam, in *Sri. Jiauddin Ahmed v. Mrs. Anwara Begum*.
28. Maulana Muhammad Ali, *The Religion of Islam* (The Ahmadiyya Anjuman Ishaat Islam, Lahore, 1990), p. 496.

29. Ali, *Religion of Islam*.
30. Ali, *Religion of Islam* (1990), pp. 496–97.
31. Justice Baharul Islam (n. 41).
32. The Fertile Crescent includes a roughly crescent-shaped area of relatively fertile land which probably had a more moderate, agriculturally productive climate in the past than today, especially in Mesopotamia and the Nile valley. Situated between the Arabian Desert to the south and the mountains of the Armenian Highland to the north, it extends from Babylonia and adjacent Elam (the southwestern province of Persia, also called Susiana) up the Tigris and Euphrates rivers to Assyria. From the Zagros Mountains east of Assyria it continues westward over Syria to the Mediterranean and extends southward to southern Palestine. The Nile valley of Egypt is often included as a further extension, especially since the short interruption in Sinai is no greater than similar desert breaks that disturb its continuity in Mesopotamia and Syria. Source: britannica.com.
33. Imam Abu Haneefah, *Al-Fiqh Al-Absat*, translated by Muhammad Huzaifah ibn Adam aal-Ebrahim (2016), archive.org, p. 3.
34. Haneefah, *Al-Fiqh Al-Absat*, p. 17.
35. Dr H. Hamid Hassan, *An Introduction to the Study of Islamic Law* (Adam Publishers & Distributors, 2010), p. 92.
36. Ibn Taymiyaah was a Hanbali jurist who emphasized on return to the original sources of Islam, the Holy Quran and the Sunnah. He believed that for any interpretation to have any authority, ijma as it may, had to be based on the two sources. Thus, he condemned the popular practices of saint worship and pilgrimages to saints' tombs which had no place in the Holy Quran and the Sunnah.
37. Fatawa; Ibn Taymiah, Vol. III, p. 141 as cited in Aqil Ahmad (n. 36), p. 176–7.
38. Syed Ameer Ali, *Muhammadan Law, Vol. 2* (Kitab Bhawan, 1986), p. 435.

Chapter 3: Indian Courts and Muslim Personal Law

1. ILR (1905) 30 BOM 537.
2. 1932 (34) BOM LR 475.
3. AIR 1971 KER 261.
4. (1981) 1 GLR3 75.
5. (2002) 7 SCC 518.
6. AIR 1971 Ker 261 (Kerala High Court).
7. (1981) 1 Gau Lr 358.
8. *Masroor Ahmed v. State (NCT of Delhi) and Another* 2008 (103) DRJ 137.
9. 2016 (1) JKJ 312.
10. 2017 (1) KLJ 1.

Chapter 4: Reforms in Islamic States

1. These figures have been extracted from the entry 'Islam by Country' available at https://en.wikipedia.org/wiki/Islam_by_country; individual sources for the figure may be sourced from the table contained therein.
2. Ronald Dworkin, *Taking Rights Seriously* (A&C Black, 2013).
3. 2014 (9) SCC 1.
4. *C. Golak Nath and Others v. State of Punjab and Another* (1967) 2 SCR 762.
5. *ADM, Jabalpur v. Shivkant Shukla* AIR 1976 SC 1207.
6. *Maneka Gandhi v. Union of India* (1978) 1 SCC 248.
7. *Suresh Kumar Koushal and Another v. Naz Foundation and Others* (2014) 1 SCC 1.
8. *Shyam Narayan Chouksey v. Union of India* (2017) 1 SCC 421.
9. *R.V. Bhasin v. State of Maharashtra* 2010 SCC OnLine Bom 31.

10. *Justice K.S. Piuttaswamy (Retd) and Another v. Union of India and Others* 2017 SCC OnLine SC 996.
11. *Binoy Viswam v. Union of India and Others* (2017) 7 SCC 59.

Chapter 5: Submissions before the Court

1. The main aim of the rule is to determine the 'mischief and defect' that the statute in question has set out to remedy, and what ruling would effectively implement this remedy. In applying the Mischief Rule, the court is essentially asking what part of the law, did the law not cover, but was meant to be rectified by the parliament in passing the bill. The intention of this rule is to make such an interpretation as shall suppress that mischief and advance the remedy. (See: GS Simhanjana, 'Literal Rule and Mischief Rule Interpretation', (*Legal Desire, 23* February 2017) <http://www.legaldesire.com/literal-rule-and-mischief-rule-interpretation/>).
2. The purposive approach sometimes referred to as purposive construction, purposive interpretation, or the "modern principle in construction" is an approach to statutory and constitutional interpretation under which common law courts interpret an enactment (that is, a statute, a part of a statute, or a clause of a constitution) in light of the purpose for which it was enacted. (See: 'Clarification – Meaning of "Purposive Interpretation"' (UPSCTree, 8 January 2017) <https://upsctree.com/2017/01/08/clarification-meaning-purposive-interpretation/>).
3. A device that is kin to the first two, in that one looks at what the intention of the Parliament was in introducing a particular piece of legislation.
4. 1897 SCC OnLine PC 14.
5. *Shamim Ara v State of UP and Another* (2002) 7 SCC 518.
6. Supra (n).

7. I (2002) DMC 11.
8. 2017 SCC OnLine Mad 74.
9. Abusaleh Sharif *'Prioritized Social Policy Options for the Women of India: Lessons from the "Triple Talaq' Fiasco"* (CRDDP, 2017).
10. *Minerva Mills Ltd. & Others v Union of India & Others* 1980 AIR 1789.
11. *Waman Rao and Others v Union Of India and Others.* (1981) 2 SCC 362.

Chapter 6: The Judgment

1. *Shayara Bano v. Union of India and Others* 2017 (7) SCJ 477.
2. (2004) 12 SCC 770.
3. *Justice K.S. Piuttaswamy (Retd) and Another v. Union of India and Others.*
4. *ADM Jabalpur.*
5. See paragraphs 228–84 of *Shayara Bano v. Union of India.*
6. *Naz Foundation* he provisions for maintenance under he judgment—Citation here are Muslim Personal Law, had Constitutional protection:ee of.
7. Peter Singer, *Animal Liberation* (Harper Collins, 2009).
8. Shiv Visvanathan, 'The Lure of the Dera' (*The Hindu*, 28 August 2017) <http://www.thehindu.com/todays-paper/tp-opinion/the-lure-of-the-dera/article19572523.ece>.
9. *Justice KS Piuttaswamy (Retd) and Another v Union of India and Others* (n).
10. N*az Foundation v. Government of NCT of Delhi and Others* 2009 (111) DRJ.
11. N*az Foundation v. Government of NCT of Delhi and Others.*
12. Filed as part of Written Submissions on behalf of the All India Muslim Law Board in *Shayara Banao,* available at http://scobserver.clpr.org.in/wp-content/uploads/2017/05/AIMPLB-latest-Affidavit-on-Triple-Talaq.pdf.

13. See *State of Gujarat v. Mirzapur Moti Kureshi Kassab Jamat and Others* (2005) 8 SCC 534.
14. Translates to 'The Disbelievers'; Surat 109 of the Holy Quran.
15. Meaning 'throne of the timeless one'; one of five takhts (seats of power) of the Sikhs.

Chapter 7: Triple Talaq Judgment Excerpts

1. Excerpts from *Shayara Bano v. Union of India and Others* 2017 (7) SCJ 477.
2. Patrick Arthur Devlin (Baron Devlin) was a British judge and Law Lord. He is well known for his part in the debate around homosexuality in Britain, where he argued contrary to his contemporary—H.L.A. Hart.

Annexure

1. Model Nikahnama taken from Dr Zeenat Shaukat Ali's book *Marriage and Divorce in Islam* (Jaico Publications Mumbai, 1987).

About the Author

Born on New Year's Day 1953 into an eminent family, Salman Khurshid had his initial education in Delhi before reading for the Bachelors of Civil Law (BCL) from St. Edmund Hall College at the University of Oxford, UK. Following his studies he stayed in Oxford at Trinity College as a Law Tutor, until he was called back to India by the Prime Minister's Office (PMO). He began his political career as an officer on special duty (in the early 1980s) in the PMO during Indira Gandhi's tenure. Since then, he has served the citizens of India as Union minister in various ministries, the last being as Minister for External Affairs (2012–14). He is the author of the bestsellers *Beyond Terrorism: New Hope for Kashmir* (1994) and *At Home in India: The Muslim Saga* (2014). He has also written the play *Sons of Babur* (2008), which has been staged in multiple countries and languages over the last decade.